Fathers Rights and the Fight for 50:50 Custody

Exposing Judicial Bias, Legal Inconsistencies, and the Case for Equal Parenting

Dera G. Madueke

This book is provided for informational and educational purposes only. Nothing contained herein should be construed as legal advice specific to your situation. Laws vary by jurisdiction, and the application of legal principles can differ depending on individual facts and circumstances. The author and publisher make no representations or warranties regarding the accuracy, completeness, or applicability of the material to your particular case.

If you require legal advice tailored to your needs, please consult a licensed attorney in your city or jurisdiction. The author and publisher expressly disclaim any liability for actions taken or not taken based on the contents of this publication.

Contents

Introduction

Family court is intended to serve as a refuge for justice and neutrality, where the best interests of the child guide every decision. It is where the law should rise above personal grievances and subjective biases. It is where the rights of parents should be respected equally, and the emotional and developmental needs of children should be safeguarded above all else. But for millions of families navigating this system today, the ideals do not match the reality.

The modern custody process is plagued by legal inconsistency, cultural bias, and structural imbalance. While every jurisdiction in the United States formally invokes the best interests of the child as the gold standard in custody decisions, there is no uniform definition of what that means. In practice, courts often rely on discretionary interpretations that differ from one courtroom to the next. This opens the door to deeply rooted presumptions and systemic inequities, especially in the treatment of fathers.

This book makes a clear and urgent case for reform. It asserts that equal custody should be the legal starting point in all child custody cases. The concept of 50:50 parenting is not radical. It is rooted in both constitutional principles and modern research in child psychology, family dynamics, and developmental health. It reflects the common sense belief that children benefit most when both of their parents are present, active, and involved in their daily lives. Equal parenting is not a gift to fathers or a concession to one party, it is a child-centered policy based on equality, fairness, and stability.

The reality is that in most jurisdictions across the United States, courts do not begin with an equal presumption. Instead, custody decisions are subject to the individual discretion of judges who are influenced by decades of legal tradition that often favors maternal custody. While there are many dedicated and impartial judges in family court, the absence of a standard default position creates a system in which outcomes are uneven and sometimes influenced by personal bias rather than legal principle.

This lack of uniformity undermines the very fabric of justice. It creates a legal landscape where parents must fight not only each other, but also the system itself. It turns co-parenting into a zero-sum battle. It burdens fathers with the impossible task of proving their right to be present in their children's lives. And it causes lasting psychological harm to children who are forced to adjust to fractured relationships and unstable living arrangements.

The consequences are not hypothetical. Decades of data confirm that children raised with equal access to both parents fare better across every measurable dimension. They perform better in school. They exhibit fewer behavioral problems. They experience lower rates of anxiety and depression. They develop stronger emotional bonds and demonstrate greater resilience in the face of stress. The evidence is overwhelming. Equal parenting works. And yet, family law continues to operate as if the status quo is acceptable.

This book is both a legal analysis and a call to action. It is written for attorneys, lawmakers, judges, and parents. It is grounded in constitutional law, supported by empirical research, and informed by real-world cases from across the country. Each chapter will explore a different aspect of the custody process, from the abuse of judicial discretion to the impact of legislative reform, from the myths surrounding fatherhood to the specific legal thresholds required to override equal custody.

We will examine landmark cases such as ***Stanley v. Illinois, 405 U.S. 645 (1972)***, ***Palmore v. Sidoti, 466 U.S. 429 (1984)***, and ***In re Marriage of LaMusga, 32 Cal. 4th 1072 (2004)*** to highlight how courts have both advanced and failed the principles of equality in custody decisions. We will review current statutes in states that have adopted equal parenting laws, such as Kentucky and Arizona, and assess how these reforms have changed custody outcomes in practice. We will analyze the arguments against 50:50 custody and provide a framework for when exceptions are not only justified but necessary.

At its core, this book makes a constitutional and moral argument. The right to parent is a fundamental liberty interest protected by the Fourteenth Amendment. That right does not vanish at the courthouse door. Unless there is compelling and verifiable evidence that one parent poses a danger or is demonstrably unfit, the law should presume that both parents have an equal role to play in their child's life.

Equal custody is not about weakening mothers or empowering fathers at their expense. It is about recognizing that parenting is not a gendered role. It is about honoring the bond between children and both of their parents. It is about rejecting outdated assumptions and building a legal system that reflects the values of fairness, equality, and child-centered care.

The time for change is now. Courts must stop treating shared parenting as an exception. Legislatures must codify equality into law. Advocates must push for reform that is evidence-based and constitutionally sound. And parents must demand a system that respects their rights and the needs of their children. This is not just a legal battle, it is a human one. And it begins with the recognition that children deserve both of their parents, equally, fully, and without condition.

ONE

The Constitutional Foundations of Parental Equality

Parenting is not a privilege given by the courts. It is a fundamental right rooted in the United States Constitution. For centuries, the legal system has recognized that parents have the natural and primary duty to raise their children. Yet, when families break apart, that right is often reshaped, or restricted, by legal systems that apply inconsistent rules, outdated assumptions, and vague standards.

This chapter lays the groundwork for the argument that **equal parenting time should be the legal starting point** in all custody cases. The reason is simple but powerful. The Constitution already supports this idea.

The Supreme Court has repeatedly affirmed that the right of parents to care for and make decisions about their children is one of the oldest and most protected liberties in American law. This right exists under the Due Process Clause of the Fourteenth Amendment, which guarantees that no person shall be deprived of life, liberty, or property without fair legal procedures. Parenting, according to the Court, is more than a biological link. It is a personal liberty.

One of the most significant cases that defines this principle is ***Troxel v. Granville, 530 U.S. 57 (2000)***. In that case, the Supreme Court struck down a Washington State law that allowed third parties, like grandparents, to petition for visitation rights, even against the wishes of a fit parent. The Court ruled that the state cannot interfere with a parent's decision unless there is strong evidence that doing so is necessary to protect the child. This ruling did not create new law. It reaffirmed what had already been established through decades of precedent. That parents have a constitutional right to make choices about how to raise their children.

So what does that mean for shared custody?

It means that if both parents are fit and willing, neither should have to fight to earn equal time with their child. The law should not allow courts to begin from a place of imbalance. Yet in most states today, there is no law requiring judges to start from a position of equal custody. Instead, judges are free to use broad discretion, which opens the door to uneven outcomes. This legal gap creates a system where one parent, often the father, must prove his worth, while the other is assumed to be the default caregiver.

That approach is not only unfair. It may be unconstitutional.

The Fourteenth Amendment was designed to prevent the state from taking away a person's rights without solid justification. If a judge denies a fit parent equal time with their child without clear evidence that it is necessary for the child's well-being, the court may be violating that parent's liberty interest. Equal custody is not about preference. It is about protection, of both parents' rights and of the child's right to strong bonds with both parents.

Legal scholars have warned that custody laws lacking a clear and consistent standard risk turning parenting into a privilege controlled by state systems rather than a right guaranteed by the Constitution. By starting every custody case with a presumption of 50:50 time-sharing, courts would align more closely with constitutional values. Any departure from equal custody should be supported by "clear and convincing evidence," the legal standard used when fundamental rights are at stake.

In short, the Constitution does not favor one parent over the other. The law, when applied fairly, should not either. We will break down the legal reasoning behind this constitutional right. We will look at the

Supreme Court's language in ***Troxel***, examine related rulings from lower courts, and explore why failing to adopt a 50:50 starting point puts both justice and children's well-being at risk.

What Does the Constitution Say About Parenting Rights

The United States Constitution does not directly mention the word "parenthood." Still, over the last century, the Supreme Court has made it clear that the right to raise and care for one's child is one of the most fundamental liberties protected under the Constitution. This right exists under the Due Process Clause of the Fourteenth Amendment, which protects individuals from government actions that interfere with their life, liberty, or property without proper legal justification.

The Court has repeatedly held that the liberty interest of parents is among the oldest recognized in constitutional law. In fact, the idea that parents have the primary responsibility and authority over their children's upbringing dates back to early American legal traditions and even to English common law.

One of the earliest and strongest rulings on this topic came in ***Meyer v. Nebraska, 262 U.S. 390 (1923)***. In that case, the Supreme Court struck down a state law that restricted foreign language education, ruling that parents have the constitutional right to control how their children are educated. This case laid the foundation for recognizing parental rights as part of personal liberty.

The Court expanded this view in ***Pierce v. Society of Sisters, 268 U.S. 510 (1925)***, when it ruled that parents could not be forced to send their children to state-run schools. The Court stated clearly that children are not "mere creatures of the state" and that it is the parents who have the right and duty to direct their upbringing and education.

These early rulings were not just about education. They were about a much broader idea that the state should not interfere in private family decisions unless there is a strong and specific reason to do so. This principle applies directly to custody cases.

The most direct ruling on parenting rights came decades later in ***Troxel v. Granville, 530 U.S. 57 (2000)***. In that case, the Supreme Court reviewed a Washington State law that allowed any person to request visitation rights with a child, even against the wishes of the child's parent. The Court ruled that this law was unconstitutional because it allowed judges to override a fit parent's decision without any proof that the parent was unfit or that the child was in danger.

The key takeaway from ***Troxel*** is that the state cannot assume control over parenting decisions simply because a judge believes they can make a better one. As long as a parent is fit, the state must defer to their judgment. The Court explained that the interest of parents in the care, custody, and control of their children is perhaps the oldest of the fundamental liberty interests recognized by American law.

If the Constitution protects a parent's right to decide who their child can visit, it also protects a parent's right to have time with their own child. That is why it is troubling that most custody cases begin without any legal presumption of equality. Fit parents should not have to prove that they deserve equal time. Instead, the court should require strong evidence before taking that time away.

In the sections ahead, we will look at how lower courts have applied these constitutional principles and why the lack of a 50:50 starting point may not only be unfair but may also violate the rights that the Supreme Court has long upheld.

The Fourteenth Amendment and the Right to Parent

The Fourteenth Amendment to the United States Constitution protects every citizen from being denied life, liberty, or property without due process of law. While the text does not specifically mention parenting, courts have long interpreted the word "liberty" to include a parent's right to care for and raise their child.

This is more than just a legal technicality. In real life, it means the government cannot take away your role as a parent, or limit it without giving you a fair hearing and a very good reason.

In custody battles, this right should matter a lot. Yet, many parents, especially fathers, feel like their right to be present in their child's life is taken away without the court giving it serious constitutional weight. Instead of starting from a position of equality, courts often begin from a place of imbalance. One parent is treated like the default, and the other, usually the father, has to prove that he deserves equal time.

This goes against the basic idea of fairness. And it may even go against the Constitution.

In ***Troxel v. Granville, 530 U.S. 57 (2000)***, the Supreme Court stated that a parent's right to direct the care, custody, and control of their child is one of the oldest and most protected liberties under American law. The court was very clear that the state cannot overrule the decisions of a fit parent simply because a judge thinks someone else's choice might be better.

That principle should apply in custody cases too. If a parent is fit and willing, there should be no need to fight just to be treated equally. The state should not get involved unless there is a real threat to the child's well-being. And when courts do interfere, they must follow the rules of due process. That means they need solid evidence, not assumptions. They need fairness, not bias.

Yet, this is not always what happens. In many cases, courts lean on tradition or instinct. They may believe they are acting in the child's best interest, but they are actually ignoring the parent's constitutional right to be treated fairly.

This chapter does not suggest that courts should be powerless to act. If one parent is unfit or poses a danger, the state has a duty to protect the child. But if both parents are fit, the court must respect their right to share in their child's life. Anything less is not just bad policy, it risks being unconstitutional.

How Courts Have Interpreted Parental Liberty

Parental liberty is not just a theoretical right. It has been defined and shaped by decades of court decisions across the United States. These rulings help us understand what the law expects when it comes to parenting and when the state is allowed to step in.

One of the earliest and most important cases is ***Meyer v. Nebraska, 262 U.S. 390 (1923)***. In this case, the Supreme Court ruled that a law banning the teaching of foreign languages in schools was unconstitutional. The Court said that parents have the right to decide how their children are educated. This decision confirmed that liberty under the Fourteenth Amendment includes the right to make important decisions about a child's upbringing.

Just two years later, in ***Pierce v. Society of Sisters, 268 U.S. 510 (1925)***, the Court ruled that parents could not be forced to send their children to public schools. The Court emphasized that the state does not own children and that it is the parent who holds the main responsibility for their care and education. The ruling made it clear that the government cannot interfere with a parent's decision without a strong and specific reason.

These cases were not about custody. But the message was clear. The Constitution protects the right of parents to raise their children in the way they believe is best. That includes decisions about education, religion, values, and living arrangements.

As time went on, this principle was extended to more family matters. In ***Stanley v. Illinois, 405 U.S. 645 (1972)***, the Supreme Court ruled that a father who was not married to the mother of his children still had the right to be heard in court before the state could declare him unfit. The Court said it is unconstitutional to take away a parent's rights just because of their marital status. The decision again pointed back to the Fourteenth Amendment and the need to protect parental liberty.

Later, in ***Troxel v. Granville, 530 U.S. 57 (2000)***, the Court faced the question of whether judges could override a fit parent's decision about who their child could spend time with. The Court said no. It ruled that the Constitution does not allow the state to step in simply because a judge thinks another choice might be better. The parent's right must be respected unless there is clear evidence that the child is in danger or being harmed.

Together, these rulings form a strong foundation. They tell us that the law sees parenting as more than a biological connection. It sees it as a protected liberty that deserves the full protection of due process. And unless there is a very good reason, the government should stay out of private family decisions.

Despite this clear history, many family courts still treat custody cases as if this constitutional principle does not apply. Fathers are often told they need to prove their value. The burden is placed on them to show why they should have equal time, even when there is no sign of abuse or neglect. That is not how constitutional liberty works. If a right is fundamental, it must be protected from the start.

Troxel v. Granville, A Turning Point in Family Law

The case of ***Troxel v. Granville, 530 U.S. 57 (2000)*** is one of the most important custody decisions ever made by the United States Supreme Court. It did not deal with a typical divorce case between two parents. Instead, it involved grandparents who wanted visitation rights. But the ruling from this case changed the way courts think about parental authority across the country.

The case began when Tommie Granville, a mother living in Washington State, limited how often her late partner's parents could visit their grandchildren. The grandparents were not happy with the new schedule. They went to court and asked a judge to give them more time with the children. Under Washington law at the time, any third party could ask for visitation rights if the court thought it was in the best interest of the child. The judge agreed with the grandparents and ordered more visits.

But Granville disagreed. She believed that as a fit and responsible parent, she had the right to make those decisions. She appealed the decision and took the case all the way to the Supreme Court.

The Supreme Court ruled in her favor. The Justices said that Washington's law gave judges too much power to interfere in private family decisions. They ruled that fit parents have a constitutional right to make choices about who their children spend time with. The government cannot simply overrule those choices just because a judge thinks another option would be better.

The Court explained that the right of parents to control the care and upbringing of their children is protected by the Constitution. They called it a fundamental liberty interest. That means it is one of the highest forms of legal protection a person can have. It is not something a court can ignore or override without a serious and proven reason.

The ruling in ***Troxel*** is important because it tells courts they must respect the decisions of fit parents. This does not mean that grandparents and others have no role. It means that courts cannot treat a parent's choices as equal to everyone else's. A judge's opinion is not enough to take away a parent's control.

So what does this mean for equal custody?

It means that when two parents are both fit and willing, courts should not pick one over the other without a very strong reason. If a judge gives more time to one parent just because they believe that parent is more nurturing or more stable without any proof that the other parent is unfit, they may be going against the Constitution.

The Court in ***Troxel*** reminded us that parenting is a personal right, not a privilege granted by a judge. Unless a parent is proven unfit or dangerous, their role in their child's life should not be limited. This is the foundation of equal parenting. It is not just a good idea. It is a constitutional principle.

Equal Custody and the Legal Presumption of Fitness

When both parents are willing and able to care for their child, the law should treat them equally. This is where the idea of **presumed fitness** comes in. If a parent has not been proven unfit by the court, they should be treated as fully capable of raising their child. This is not just a matter of fairness. It is a matter of constitutional protection.

Many courts say they follow the best interests of the child standard. But they often begin the case with no legal presumption of equality between the parents. Instead, the judge is allowed to decide what seems best based on their own experience, beliefs, or even personal instincts. That kind of freedom may sound useful in theory, but in reality, it has led to uneven and often biased outcomes.

A true legal presumption means that equal custody is the starting point. The court must assume both parents are fit and equally important in the child's life unless someone presents strong and clear evidence to prove otherwise. This is what legal professionals call the burden of proof. Whoever wants to reduce a fit parent's time must provide evidence that shows doing so is necessary to protect the child.

In many custody cases today, this process is reversed. Fathers especially find themselves in the position of having to prove their worth from the beginning. This is not just a personal struggle. It is a structural flaw in the legal system.

Let us look at this from the perspective of the Supreme Court's decision in ***Troxel v. Granville, 530 U.S. 57 (2000)***. In that ruling, the Court made it clear that the government does not have the authority to override a fit parent's decisions without strong justification. If that is true for a mother's decision about grandparents, then it should also apply when the court is deciding how much time a father is allowed to have with his own child. Anything less undermines the very liberty the Court sought to protect.

This is where we must go beyond case law and offer real-world reform.

A smart and balanced custody law would begin with a simple rule. If both parents are fit and involved, the court must start at 50:50. Only then should the judge consider specific evidence that could justify a different arrangement. This kind of law would still allow courts to protect children in cases involving abuse, instability, or danger. But it would no longer allow unproven bias or vague opinions to take the place of evidence.

Another idea worth considering is requiring a formal finding of unfitness before any parent is denied equal time. This means the court would need to issue a clear ruling that explains why one parent is not capable of sharing custody. This ruling would have to be based on facts presented in court, not just general impressions.

Finally, states could require courts to provide written explanations when equal custody is not ordered. These explanations should be part of the official record and open to appeal. This would create accountability and make sure that judges cannot quietly apply personal preferences without being questioned.

In summary, the Constitution protects parenting as a liberty interest. That protection means something. It requires courts to begin with the assumption that both parents matter equally. Anything less is not only unfair. It may be unlawful.

Why the Burden of Proof Must Be on Those Who Challenge Equal Parenting

In every area of law, the party seeking to limit or remove another person's rights carries the burden of proof. This is a foundational principle of justice. It exists to protect people from losing their freedom without evidence, from being punished without reason, and from being silenced without a hearing. The same must apply to parenting. If a court is going to reduce a fit parent's access to their own child, that decision must be supported by clear and convincing proof. Nothing less should ever be allowed.

In custody cases, however, we see something very different. The system often assumes that one parent will become the primary caregiver, and the other parent must fight to prove they deserve equal time. This process reverses the proper legal order. It places the burden of proof on the wrong person. A parent who has done nothing wrong is treated like a visitor in their child's life until they convince the court otherwise. This is not due process. It is a legal shortcut dressed up as custom.

The question we must now ask is this. If the Constitution protects the liberty of parents, why does family court so often ignore that when custody is on the line?

The answer lies in the culture of family law. Courts have relied so heavily on the phrase "best interest of the child" that they have built a legal structure around it that operates without fixed rules. What began as a noble goal has become a vague and open-ended license to decide parenting rights based on instinct rather than legal principle. In the absence of a legal presumption in favor of shared custody, courts are allowed to make unequal decisions based on whatever they personally believe is best.

This is dangerous. It opens the door to bias. It closes the door to accountability. And it creates a structure where a parent can be pushed aside without being found unfit.

What should we do about it?

Here are some new, bold, and necessary ideas that could completely change how the burden of proof works in custody cases.

First, courts should be required by statute to begin every custody case with a written declaration of parental fitness for both parents. This would not be a judgment. It would be a statement that until evidence is presented to show otherwise, both parents are presumed capable and safe. This simple act would reshape how lawyers argue, how judges think, and how parents approach their case. It would shift the culture away from competition and toward cooperation.

Second, courts should not be allowed to deny equal time unless the challenging party provides documented proof of danger, abuse, instability, or severe unavailability. This documentation should meet a clear standard. Police records, mental health evaluations, substance abuse histories, or specific medical evidence should be the minimum level of proof. Mere accusations, emotional testimony, or assumptions about gender roles should not be accepted.

Third, the law should require that any custody plan that deviates from 50:50 be accompanied by a written judicial finding that explains, in detail, why equal time was not granted. This finding should be public unless sealed for safety reasons. It should cite facts presented in court and reference applicable law. Most importantly, it should be subject to automatic review by a higher court within a fixed timeline. This would create real oversight and make it much harder for silent bias to control outcomes.

Fourth, states should implement something we might call a Parenting Equity Certification. This would be a professional training and examination program required for all family court judges before they can preside over custody cases. The training would focus on understanding unconscious bias, reviewing modern developmental psychology, and learning about updated family dynamics. This certification should be renewed every five years, and complaints about decisions that show consistent imbalance should trigger a review of the judge's record.

Fifth, every state should create an independent Office for Parenting Rights Review. This office would function like a public legal ombudsman. Its sole purpose would be to review complaints from parents who believe their rights were unjustly limited. It would have the authority to request transcripts, audit decision trends, and recommend legislative or procedural reform. In other words, it would be a watchdog focused on the fairness of custody determinations.

Sixth, the system should recognize and apply a principle we can call Parental Equity by Default. This principle would be written into law and would state that in the absence of strong contrary evidence, equal parenting time is the default standard in all custody cases. Courts would be required to start from this position and move away from it only when justified. Just as in criminal law where the presumption is innocence, in family law the presumption should be parental equality.

Let us pause and reflect on how different custody court would feel if these structures were in place. Fathers would no longer begin as outsiders. Mothers would no longer carry the full weight of caregiving by assumption. Children would not have to endure the confusion of split loyalty and uneven access. Judges would not be left alone with unlimited discretion but would be guided by clear rules and real oversight.

This is how you protect both fairness and freedom. You start by placing the burden where it belongs. If someone wants to take away a parent's time, they must prove why. If they cannot, the court must not let that time be taken.

TWO

Judicial Discretion Versus Equal Presumption, The Battle Over the Best Interests Standard

In American family law, no phrase is more frequently used or more poorly defined than the best interests of the child. It appears in every state's custody statute and in nearly every custody ruling. Judges cite it as the reason for their decisions. Lawyers build entire arguments around it. Parents are told it is the standard that governs who their child lives with and how often they will see them. But despite its popularity, the phrase remains vague, inconsistent, and deeply subjective.

The concept itself is not new. The best interests doctrine was first recognized by American courts in the early nineteenth century as part of the move away from the father-centered custody model known as the paternal preference. This shift was driven by changes in family roles, evolving views on childhood development, and the influence of maternal presumption in early equity courts. Today, all fifty states use the best interests test as the standard for deciding custody and visitation. However, the way courts apply it varies widely.

Most state laws include a list of factors for judges to consider. These typically include the emotional bonds between parent and child, each parent's ability to meet the child's needs, the stability of each home, and the mental and physical health of the parents. Some states include additional factors like the child's preference, parental history of domestic violence, and the willingness of each parent to support the child's relationship with the other parent. For example, Section 402 of the California Family Code lists more than a dozen different considerations. In contrast, Texas Family Code Section 153.002 provides a very broad guideline and gives the court wide discretion.

But the problem is that these lists are guidelines, not rules. They are not ranked in importance. Judges are free to interpret and weigh them however they choose. This gives them broad discretionary power that is rarely checked by higher courts. And while discretion allows for flexibility, it also opens the door to inconsistency and unspoken bias.

The result is a system in which two equally fit and loving parents can receive vastly different outcomes depending on the county, the courtroom, or the individual judge. A 2014 report by the National Parents Organization analyzed custody statutes in all fifty states and found that only a few encouraged equal parenting time as a starting point. Most gave judges open-ended authority to define best interests on a case-by-case basis. This has created wide variation not just between states, but within them.

Studies have shown that this variation often disfavors fathers. A comprehensive analysis published in the *Journal of Divorce and Remarriage* found that mothers were awarded primary physical custody in over 70% of contested cases, even when no evidence of unfitness or risk was present. In these cases, courts relied heavily on tradition and judicial interpretation of best interests, not on measurable evidence that one parent was more capable.

This is where the issue becomes legal, not just practical. When a judge can decide that one parent should have limited access to their child without a clear standard or a required burden of proof, that decision may infringe on a constitutional right. As we saw in ***Troxel v. Granville, 530 U.S. 57 (2000)***, the Supreme Court recognized that parents have a fundamental liberty interest in the care, custody, and control of their children. That right cannot be taken away based on preference or assumption. It requires compelling evidence and due process.

In ***Palmore v. Sidoti, 466 U.S. 429 (1984)***, the Court warned that even well-meaning custody decisions cannot be justified by the influence of social bias or public opinion. The Florida court in that case had removed a child from the mother after she entered an interracial relationship, claiming that the child might suffer from societal prejudice. The Supreme Court struck the decision down, stating that the Constitution does not allow the law to give effect to private biases. While the facts of that case were specific, the principle is broad. Courts must base their decisions on law and evidence, not personal views or cultural pressures.

And yet, in custody courts today, that line is still crossed. Judges are not required to write detailed findings when they rule against shared parenting. Their decisions are rarely appealed because custody rulings are considered fact-based and appellate courts often defer to the trial judge. The result is a system where power is concentrated in a single voice, without consistent standards and without oversight.

This is not an attack on judges. There are judges who work with care and concern for the children before them. But no system should rely on the personal character of its officials. The law must provide structure. It must start from equality and move only when evidence demands it. Equal parenting should not be requested. It should be the presumption. If someone seeks to depart from it, they should carry the burden of proof and present clear facts that support the change.

What Is the Best Interests Standard

The best interests of the child. It is the phrase that decides everything in a custody case. It is the line every judge, lawyer, and social worker repeats. But what does it really mean? And how is it actually used in courtrooms?

At its core, the best interests standard is supposed to guide courts toward outcomes that protect a child's health, safety, and emotional development. The idea is to give judges the freedom to look at the unique details of each family and decide what arrangement works best for the child. That sounds good in theory. But the truth is more complicated.

In most states, the law does not give one clear definition of what the best interests are, but it offers a list of possible factors. These include things like the emotional ties between the child and each parent, the ability of each parent to provide a stable home, the mental and physical health of the parents, and how well the parents can cooperate with each other. Some states add more. Some leave it vague.

That is where problems begin. When a law gives too many possible answers and no clear rule, it becomes easy for judges to rely on their own opinions rather than the facts. For example, one judge might think that a parent working full time cannot provide emotional support. Another might believe that staying at home makes someone more nurturing. Neither of these views is necessarily correct. But if the law allows it, those beliefs can shape custody decisions without real evidence.

And the effect of that is serious. Families can walk into court with the exact same facts and walk out with completely different outcomes, depending on which judge hears the case. A father who lives five minutes away, attends every school event, and has no history of abuse or instability may still be given every other weekend while the mother is granted full-time custody. Not because of any wrongdoing, but because the judge believes that is what is best. When discretion is this wide, it becomes unpredictable. And when it is unpredictable, it becomes unfair.

I believe the best interests standard can work, but only if it is applied within a clear legal framework that begins with equal parenting. If both parents are fit and involved, the starting point must be equal time. From there, the court can look at specific facts that may require adjustments. But the adjustment must come from evidence, not assumption.

Take for example a situation where both parents live in the same school district. The child has a strong relationship with both. One parent works during the day. The other works evenings. Instead of assuming one should have primary custody, the court could adopt a shared week schedule that rotates evenings and weekends to match the work hours of each parent. That way, both parents stay involved and the child's routine remains stable.

In another situation, imagine both parents are loving and present, but they have a high level of conflict. This often leads judges to favor one parent, thinking that giving full custody to one will reduce the tension. But research tells us otherwise. Studies show that children do not benefit from losing access to a parent just because the parents cannot get along. Instead, courts could create a parenting plan that reduces direct communication, uses apps for scheduling, and provides mediation support as needed. The conflict is managed, not used as an excuse to remove a parent.

There is also the issue of mental health. Suppose one parent has been diagnosed with anxiety but is undergoing treatment and has a strong support system. Too often, courts view any mental health history as a red flag. But that is not fair or helpful. Instead, the court should look at how the parent is functioning, whether the condition affects parenting, and whether it is being responsibly managed. Equal time should not be denied based on a diagnosis alone.

These examples show how the best interests standard can still work if the court starts from equality and only shifts based on clear facts.

Judges need better tools. Instead of being asked to guess what is best, they should be given a clear default. Equal parenting should be that default. That way, judges are not deciding from scratch every time. They are starting from a position that respects both parents and protects the child's right to meaningful relationships with both.

To make this work, the law must change. It must define best interests in a way that respects constitutional rights. It must require courts to explain their decisions. And it must give both parents equal footing from the beginning.

Looking Beyond What Sounds Simple and Fair

On the surface, the best interests of the child sounds like the most reasonable and protective idea in all of family law. Who would argue against doing what is best for a child? It feels like common sense. It is meant to be neutral. It is supposed to rise above the conflict between parents and keep the focus where it belongs.

But when you look more closely at how the phrase is used in real courtrooms, you begin to see the cracks in its surface. You begin to understand how a term that sounds fair can actually lead to unfair outcomes. The best interests standard is supposed to protect children, but in too many cases, it ends up protecting the assumptions of adults.

One of the biggest problems is that the standard has no single meaning. Judges are given a list of factors to consider, but they are not required to explain how those factors are weighed or how the decision was reached. This opens the door to personal beliefs and unconscious bias. One judge might believe that young children belong with their mothers. Another might believe that children need only one stable home instead of rotating between two. These beliefs are not written into the law. They are often inherited from culture, tradition, or habit.

As a result, two families with nearly identical facts can walk into two different courtrooms and walk out with opposite custody arrangements. That should never happen in a system that claims to be based on law. Predictability is a key part of justice. Without it, rights become suggestions. And in family court, this means that parenting time becomes negotiable based on personality and perspective rather than law and evidence.

Here is another concern. In many cases, the best interests standard becomes a way to justify unequal parenting rather than prevent harm. Courts sometimes argue that it is better for the child to stay in one home most of the time for the sake of stability. But research consistently shows that children do not suffer from spending time in two homes. What they suffer from is the loss of regular access to a parent. It is not the schedule that harms them. It is the separation from one half of their family life.

So what should the best interests standard actually mean?

We believe it is time to redefine it. Not just for judges. Not just for lawyers. But for society as a whole.

The best interests of the child must start with the assumption that a child needs both parents equally when both parents are fit, loving, and available. It must not be assumed that one parent is better suited simply because of gender, income, or past roles during the relationship. Children do not measure love by paychecks or chores. They measure love by presence and consistency.

A better definition of the best interests of the child would look something like this:

The best interests of the child means a custody arrangement that allows the child to maintain strong, continuous, and meaningful relationships with both parents while ensuring the child's physical safety, emotional security, developmental stability, and cultural identity. This presumes equal time with both parents unless clear and convincing evidence proves that such an arrangement would cause serious harm to the child.

This definition is not vague. It is not based on feeling. It is rooted in child development research, constitutional rights, and practical parenting realities.

Let us explore why each part of that definition matters.

First, the focus on strong and continuous relationships with both parents reflects what decades of research has shown. Children do best when they have equal access to both of their parents. They perform better in school. They have lower rates of anxiety and depression. They form healthier relationships as adults. This is not speculation. These are the findings of studies published in peer-reviewed journals across multiple countries.

Second, the idea of physical safety and emotional security is key. Equal parenting must never be given when there is abuse, neglect, or active danger. But in cases where both parents are fit, love their children, and can provide safe homes, time should not be restricted based on routine discomforts or inconvenience.

Third, developmental stability means more than just having a fixed bedroom. It means having dependable access to both parents, being allowed to attach to both without guilt, and being raised without being pulled into adult conflict. A child who sees both parents regularly knows they are not being forced to choose sides. That is true emotional stability.

Fourth, cultural identity is often overlooked. A child may come from a household with specific religious, racial, or cultural traditions. When one parent is excluded, that entire part of the child's identity can be weakened. Best interest must include the whole child, not just their schedule or school district.

And finally, requiring clear and convincing evidence before rejecting equal custody brings the standard in line with other areas of serious rights protection. In criminal cases, we use beyond a reasonable doubt. In civil cases with serious personal consequences, we use clear and convincing evidence. If we use those high standards to protect money or liberty, surely we must use them to protect a child's bond with a parent.

We must stop letting the best interests standard become a polite excuse for imbalance. We must stop using tradition as a substitute for truth. And we must challenge the idea that judges can protect children without first respecting their relationships with both parents.

The best interests of the child must mean more than stability for one parent. It must mean stability with both. Not just for a weekend. Not just for a holiday. But as the starting point of a healthy, fair, and constitutional life.

How Judicial Discretion Leads to Unequal Results

Judicial discretion in family court means that judges have the freedom to make decisions based on the facts of each case. This is often described as a strength of the system. It allows judges to consider each family's unique circumstances. It gives them flexibility. It is supposed to keep custody decisions fair and child focused.

But when discretion is too broad and left without structure, it stops being fair. It becomes unpredictable. It allows for uneven results, even when the facts of different cases are nearly identical. In custody law, that unpredictability often leads to inequality. And in many cases, the inequality falls hardest on fathers.

Let us look at what this means in practice.

Imagine two parents going through a custody dispute. Both have been involved in their child's life since birth. Both live within the same school district. There are no safety concerns, no criminal records, no evidence of neglect, and no major conflict between them. In theory, they should each walk out of court with a parenting schedule that reflects equality.

But in courtroom after courtroom, across state after state, what happens instead is very different. The mother is awarded primary physical custody. The father receives alternating weekends, maybe one midweek dinner visit. And unless he fights the ruling on appeal, that becomes his life for the next several years.

This is not a rare case. It is the standard result in many courts.

A 2019 study by Custody X Change, a company that analyzes parenting time data, found that in over seventy percent of contested custody cases, mothers were awarded more parenting time than fathers. In several states, including New York, Illinois, and California, the average parenting time for fathers was below thirty percent. These results were not tied to findings of abuse or unfitness. They were simply outcomes based on the judge's decision.

That is the problem with unstructured discretion. It allows personal opinions and assumptions to guide legal decisions. A judge might believe, even unconsciously, that young children belong with their mothers. Another might assume that because a father works longer hours, he cannot parent effectively. These are not legal standards. They are personal views. And they shape real lives.

When the law does not require a judge to begin from equal parenting, the outcome becomes a matter of personality. Judges who support shared custody may give it freely. Judges who do not believe in it may never allow it. This is not how rights are supposed to work. A parent's time with their child should not depend on the zip code of the courthouse.

This is where change is needed.

Discretion should not be eliminated. But it should be guided. Courts need a clear starting point. They need a presumption of equal parenting when both parents are fit. This creates balance. It sets a standard. It does not remove the judge's power. It simply channels that power toward fairness.

With equal parenting as the default, a judge who wants to limit one parent's time would have to explain why. They would need to cite facts. They would need to show how the decision protects the child. That kind of explanation adds transparency and gives the losing parent a clear record to appeal.

More importantly, it forces courts to focus on actual harm rather than general beliefs.

For example, if one parent has a history of moving frequently, the court might reduce overnight time for the sake of the child's stability. But that decision would need to be documented. It would have to connect the parent's behavior to the child's best interest in a specific way.

Another example involves high conflict between the parents. Often, courts believe that giving one parent primary custody will reduce the conflict. But research shows the opposite. Children benefit more from continued contact with both parents than from reduced parental disagreement. Courts should be encouraged to order communication tools, co-parenting classes, or parallel parenting schedules instead of simply removing one parent from the child's life.

The truth is that discretion without guidance becomes power without boundaries. And in family court, that power is often exercised without anyone truly challenging it.

Judges are not above criticism. But they also work in a system that asks them to make emotional decisions without giving them the right tools. It is not enough to ask judges to do their best. The law must define what the best means. And that definition must begin with the understanding that both parents matter, both have rights, and both are necessary in the life of a child.

The Hidden Role of Gender Assumptions in Court

Family court is one of the few places in the legal system where silent stereotypes still shape outcomes more than most people realize. In theory, custody decisions are made without bias. In theory, judges are neutral and apply the law fairly. But in practice, gender assumptions often creep into the courtroom and influence who gets custody, who gets time, and who gets sidelined.

These assumptions are rarely spoken out loud. They often come dressed in polite language. A judge might say that one parent offers more consistency. Or that the child is more emotionally connected to the parent who has been the primary caregiver. Or that moving back and forth between homes would be too disruptive. These statements sound reasonable. But underneath, they often reflect old beliefs about gender roles.

One of the most common assumptions is that mothers are naturally better caregivers. This belief has deep roots. For much of the twentieth century, family law operated under the tender years doctrine. That rule stated that young children should stay with their mothers unless there was strong evidence of harm. Though this doctrine is no longer part of formal law in most states, its influence remains in the way some judges think about parenting.

Many courts still expect mothers to be more nurturing and emotionally available. At the same time, they expect fathers to be secondary, less involved, or less capable of handling the emotional and daily needs of a child. These beliefs often go unchallenged because they are built into the culture of custody court.

The effects are seen in the data. As noted in a 2020 report by the United States Census Bureau, over 80% of custodial parents in single-parent homes are mothers. In contested custody cases, even when both parents are present and active, courts still award primary physical custody to mothers in the majority of cases. This is not because mothers are always more fit. It is often because courts continue to act as if parenting is a mother's job first and a father's job second.

This bias can show up in subtle ways. A mother who misses a school event might be seen as overwhelmed. A father who misses the same event might be seen as disinterested. A mother who cries during testimony may be viewed as passionate. A father who shows the same emotion may be seen as unstable. These are not legal rules. They are judgments made by people who are supposed to apply the law without favor.

Even when judges do not intend to be biased, their decisions can still be shaped by cultural expectations. A 2018 study published in the *Family Court Review* found that judges often default to traditional roles when making decisions in cases where the facts are balanced. That means even when there is no evidence that one parent is more capable, courts may still lean toward the parent who handled more caregiving during the marriage. That parent is usually the mother.

But roles in families have changed. In today's world, many fathers are deeply involved in their children's lives. They change diapers, attend parent-teacher meetings, cook meals, and know their child's emotional needs. Many mothers work full-time, just like fathers do. The old division of labor no longer fits the way families actually live.

Courts need to catch up.

Instead of assuming roles based on past norms, courts should evaluate what each parent does now and what each parent can continue to do after separation. That evaluation should not favor the past if the future clearly supports equal involvement.

Imagine a father who took on a smaller caregiving role during the marriage because the mother stayed home. After separation, both parents adjust their schedules and commit to equal time. The court should look forward, not backward. It should support a parenting plan that reflects where the family is going, not where it used to be.

Another example is a mother who worked full-time and had less time during the weekdays. After separation, she may want to rebalance the schedule to spend more time with her child. That choice should be respected too. The goal is not to lock parents into their past roles. The goal is to build a custody plan that allows both parents to fully engage in raising their child.

We must also reject the idea that equal parenting is a threat to stability. A child who has strong bonds with both parents is not confused by a shared schedule. That child is supported. That child knows they are not being asked to choose. That child grows up knowing both parents are fully present.

Gender assumptions are not always obvious. They do not always come from bad intentions. But they still harm families. They still limit fathers. They still overburden mothers. And they still keep courts from doing what is truly best for children.

Lessons from Palmore v. Sidoti and LaMusga

Court decisions carry weight not only because of their immediate outcomes but because of the legal messages they send. In custody law, two cases stand out for the lessons they offer on how courts deal with bias, discretion, and the best interests of the child. These cases are not identical in facts or time period, but when placed side by side, they reveal something powerful. They show how the law struggles to balance fairness, cultural influence, and the real-life needs of families.

The first case is ***Palmore v. Sidoti, 466 U.S. 429 (1984)***. The facts were simple but deeply troubling. A white mother in Florida was awarded custody of her child after divorce. Later, she entered a relationship with a Black man and moved in with him. The father of the child returned to court and asked for custody. He argued that the child would face social stigma and emotional harm because of the interracial household. Shockingly, the trial court agreed and transferred custody to the father. The reason was not based on unfitness or danger. It was based on a belief that society's prejudice could harm the child and that avoiding that harm was a valid reason to remove the child from the mother's home.

The case reached the United States Supreme Court. The Court unanimously reversed the lower court. In its ruling, the Court acknowledged that private bias exists in society, but it firmly stated that the Constitution does not permit the government to give effect to those biases. Doing so would violate the Equal Protection Clause. The Court explained that even if the judge acted with good intentions, the decision was still rooted in prejudice and therefore unconstitutional.

This case is often cited in law schools to teach equal protection. But in family court, its deeper lesson is sometimes ignored. ***Palmore*** teaches that custody decisions must be based on individual fitness and child well-being, not social discomfort or cultural bias. That includes bias about gender, race, class, or family structure. If a judge allows personal or societal prejudice to guide their decision, that ruling cannot stand.

The second case is ***In re Marriage of LaMusga, 32 Cal. 4th 1072 (2004)***, a much more recent and controversial decision from the California Supreme Court. In this case, the mother wished to relocate with her children to another state. The father objected, arguing that the move would damage his relationship with the children. The trial court agreed and denied the relocation. The appellate court reversed, but the California Supreme Court reinstated the trial court's decision. The court held that the potential harm to the relationship between the child and the nonmoving parent is a valid factor in denying relocation, even if the moving parent is not unfit.

On the surface, this may seem like a fair balance. But when viewed more closely, it raises important concerns about how the best interests standard is applied. ***LaMusga*** allows courts to stop a parent from moving not because they are dangerous or unfit, but because their move might reduce contact with the other parent. That reasoning, while well-meaning, gives courts a high level of control over personal choices and can put one parent in a position where they must choose between their freedom and their relationship with their child.

What both cases show is that courts can and do act with discretion that goes beyond clear danger or unfitness. Sometimes that discretion is used to protect a child from bias. Sometimes it is used to limit a parent's autonomy in the name of stability. In both cases, we are reminded that broad discretion must always be checked by the Constitution and by reason.

What should we take from this?

First, judges must be trained to recognize their own assumptions. In ***Palmore***, the judge may have thought they were acting in the child's best interest, but they were really reinforcing racism. In many modern custody cases, judges may believe they are preserving stability, when in fact they are reinforcing outdated ideas about parenting roles. Courts should be required to write down their reasoning and explain how it is connected to real evidence, not general ideas.

Second, custody decisions should never be allowed to drift into personal judgment. In ***LaMusga***, the decision turned on what the judge believed might happen to the parent-child relationship. There was no certain harm. Just possibility. That kind of decision-making, while common in family court, must be restrained by evidence. Courts should not act on what might go wrong. They must act on what has gone wrong or is clearly about to go wrong.

Third, family courts must recognize that relationships are living things. They grow. They adjust. They change based on effort, not geography alone. Denying a move or limiting custody must not be based on fear of what could be lost, but on proof that a parent cannot or will not keep their bond strong. Technology, travel, shared schedules, and creativity all offer ways for families to stay connected. Courts should consider those tools before restricting a parent's rights.

These two cases: ***Palmore*** and ***LaMusga*** show how deeply human custody law really is. They show that even courts trying to do the right thing can make decisions that fail to honor equality. And they show that the best interests of the child cannot be separated from the rights of the parents.

Why Equal Presumption Is a More Reliable Starting Point

Every custody case begins with a question. What arrangement will be best for the child? It sounds simple, but the way that question is answered depends entirely on where the court begins. If a court starts with the idea that one parent should have primary custody and the other should be given limited time, the process becomes a competition. Each parent is forced to prove why they deserve more. Every strength is turned into an argument. Every weakness is used as a weapon.

Now imagine a different beginning. One where the court starts from a position that both parents matter equally. One where equal time is assumed, not argued for. One where the burden of proof is placed on the person who wants to reduce that time. This is what we mean by equal presumption.

Equal presumption means that unless there is a strong and clear reason to do otherwise, both parents should be given equal parenting time. It does not mean courts cannot adjust schedules. It does not mean safety concerns are ignored. It means that the law respects both parents as essential from the very start.

There are several reasons why this approach is not only fair but also more effective.

First, equal presumption honors the constitutional rights of parents. As seen in ***Troxel v. Granville, 530 U.S. 57 (2000)***, the Supreme Court recognized that parents have a fundamental liberty interest in the care and custody of their children. That interest does not disappear when two parents separate. Starting with equal parenting respects that liberty and avoids making one parent prove their worth just to stay involved.

Second, equal presumption protects children from the emotional harm of losing one parent. Studies from the American Psychological

Association and other research bodies have shown that children who have strong relationships with both parents after divorce tend to be healthier emotionally and socially. They experience fewer behavioral problems. They perform better in school. They show greater resilience over time. These benefits are most clearly seen when both parents are deeply involved, not just visiting occasionally.

Third, equal presumption reduces conflict between parents. When courts do not start with equality, they create a fight. Parents are told that one will win more time and one will get less. That dynamic turns co-parents into opponents. But when both parents know they will begin from equal ground, the pressure to compete fades. They are more likely to focus on cooperation. They are more likely to build parenting plans that work for their child rather than plans built to win a legal battle.

Fourth, equal presumption makes the legal system more predictable and more just. Right now, outcomes vary from courtroom to courtroom. Some judges prefer shared custody. Others do not. This inconsistency creates confusion and mistrust. It leaves families feeling that the process is a gamble. But a law that clearly states equal time is the default brings clarity. It gives families and lawyers a starting point that is grounded in fairness.

Let us be clear: Equal presumption is not about rigid formulas. It is not about forcing a schedule where it does not fit. It is about where the court begins, not where it must end. If there is evidence that equal time will harm the child or that one parent is unable or unwilling to provide safe care, then the court can and should make a different ruling. But the key is evidence. Not assumptions. Not tradition. Not convenience.

Let us consider how this works in real life.

A judge sees two parents standing before them. Both are employed. Both have a history of involvement in the child's life. Both live nearby. But one parent took on more daily care during the relationship, perhaps because the other worked longer hours. In the old model, that parent might be awarded primary custody based on history. But under equal presumption, the court would look forward. It would ask what each parent is able and willing to do now. It would not punish a parent for working outside the home. It would not reward the other simply for being available more often in the past.

Another common scenario involves claims that a shared schedule would be too hard for the child. But that claim must be backed by facts. It is not enough to say that switching homes is disruptive. Children are incredibly adaptable when the change is managed with care. What is truly disruptive is feeling disconnected from one parent. Equal time helps prevent that. The court's job is to help make that balance possible, not to avoid it because it requires effort.

Equal presumption also sends a strong message. It tells children that both parents are important. It tells mothers they are not alone in raising their children. It tells fathers they are not outsiders. It tells society that parenting is not a competition of roles. It is a partnership in responsibility.

This is not just good law. It is good policy. It creates better outcomes for children, more trust in the legal system, and brings family law in line with modern family life.

THREE

Fathers in Family Court, The Systemic Barriers to Equal Custody

When most people hear the words family court, they think of a place where justice is tailored to the needs of children. A place where love and responsibility are valued over money and status. A place where the law listens carefully and gives every parent a fair chance. But for many fathers, that is not what family court feels like. It feels like a door they must knock on over and over again. It feels like a system that sees them as optional. And it feels like a place where they must prove they belong in their own child's life.

This chapter is not an emotional appeal. It is not based on frustration alone. It is based on evidence. It is based on decades of data, court trends, and the lived experience of fathers across the country. It is based on the recognition that while the law has evolved, the system still holds on to old habits. And one of those habits is seeing fathers as less essential than mothers when it comes to caregiving.

Let us begin with what the law says.

The United States Supreme Court has made it clear that the Constitution protects the parental rights of fathers as much as mothers. In ***Stanley v. Illinois, 405 U.S. 645 (1972)***, the Court ruled that an unmarried father could not be denied custody of his children simply because he was not married to their mother. The Court said the state must treat him as a parent and give him a chance to prove his fitness before taking away his rights. The decision emphasized that parental rights are based on biology and commitment, not on marital status.

This was a major step forward. It acknowledged that a father's role is not created by paperwork but by presence and care. But while this ruling changed the law, it did not fully change the culture inside family courtrooms.

Even today, many fathers find themselves starting from behind. They are often expected to ask for permission to parent. They are expected to explain how they will make time, how they will manage school pickups, how they will handle discipline, meals, and bedtime routines. These are fair questions. But when those same questions are not asked with the same weight to mothers, the process becomes unfair.

There is also a social script that plays out quietly. It goes something like this. The mother is the natural caregiver. The father is the backup. If he is very involved, he gets praise. If he is not, he is forgotten. The court rarely asks whether the mother will support the father's role. But it often asks whether the father will support the mother. This imbalance is not written into law, but it shows up in how the law is applied.

Research backs this up. A 2018 study published in the *Journal of Divorce and Remarriage* showed that even when fathers requested shared custody, they received it in less than half of the cases. This was true even when no safety or stability issues were present. Another report by the National Parents Organization gave over twenty states a failing grade in custody fairness, noting that most still default to primary custody for one parent and limited time for the other.

This pattern has consequences. Children lose daily connection with their fathers. Fathers become weekend visitors in their own children's lives. Mothers are left carrying a heavier parenting load than they may want or need. And courts are flooded with modification requests, enforcement issues, and emotional strain that could have been avoided with a more balanced approach from the start.

So what causes this imbalance to continue?

Part of it is tradition. For years, the standard family model involved the mother at home and the father at work. Courts were built around that model. Even as more families share responsibilities equally, the system has been slow to adapt.

Part of it is the best interests standard. As we explored in the last chapter, this standard gives judges wide freedom to make decisions based on what they believe is right. Without clear rules or a presumption of equality, many judges fall back on traditional roles.

And part of it is a misunderstanding of what fathers can and do bring to the lives of their children. Courts may view fathers as less emotional, less organized, or less nurturing. But those views are based on stereotypes, not evidence. Fathers are caregivers. They offer structure, discipline, play, encouragement, protection, and love. Their role is not less. It is simply different. And that difference is essential.

Let us also be honest. There are fathers who do not show up. There are fathers who fail to take responsibility. But the same is true of some mothers. Uninvolved parenting is not a gendered issue. It is a human issue. Courts must look at the facts of each case, not the expectations of society.

To fix this, we need more than new laws. We need new thinking.

Courts should start with the idea that both parents are equally important. That both are capable of care. That both deserve a meaningful role. Parenting plans should reflect this from the first hearing, not after a legal battle. Judges should be trained to spot their own bias. Legal education should include modern research on fatherhood. And states should publish custody data by gender, so we can track outcomes and hold the system accountable.

This is not just about fathers. It is about fairness. It is about children. It is about recognizing that love and commitment are not defined by gender. They are defined by presence, consistency, and sacrifice.

Stories from Real Courtrooms Across America

Behind every custody ruling is a story. A real parent. A real child. A family trying to adjust to a new version of itself. These stories reveal the human side of what legal terms like primary custody, best interest, or parenting time often hide. They also reveal the patterns that data alone cannot explain. They show how fathers across the country are stepping into court expecting fairness but are often met with a system that does not always recognize their full value.

Let us begin with a case from Georgia. A father who had been actively involved in his daughter's life since birth appeared in court after separating from the mother. He had a stable job, lived fifteen minutes from the child's school, and shared transportation duties even after the breakup. When he requested equal time, the judge asked him why he thought he deserved it. The judge then awarded primary custody to the mother without any finding of unfitness or danger on the father's part. The ruling gave him every other weekend and one overnight per week.

The father appealed. He argued that the court had made no negative findings about his parenting. But the appellate court upheld the decision, citing judicial discretion and the best interests of the child. Nowhere in the ruling did the court explain how that limited time supported the child's development more than a balanced plan would have.

A second example comes from Illinois. In this case, the father was the stay-at-home parent for the first three years of the child's life while the mother worked full-time. After the separation, both parents requested shared custody. But the court ruled in favor of the mother, stating that the child needed more emotional consistency and that it would be too disruptive to move between homes. The judge noted that while the father had been the primary caregiver, the child would now need to transition into a more structured setting with the mother.

The decision was difficult to understand. The father had not changed his availability. There was no evidence of harm. Yet the court chose to create a new routine instead of preserving the one that already existed.

The ruling seemed to favor a more traditional structure over the actual facts of the case.

In California, a father who had joint legal custody requested a 50:50 physical schedule when his son entered middle school. The mother objected, claiming the child would fall behind in school with two homes. The father presented data, academic reports, and even letters from teachers showing that the child was thriving with regular contact. But the judge ruled against him, saying that in her experience, children at that age need one home base to succeed. The father's petition was denied without any finding of harm or risk. The decision was based on belief, not evidence.

These stories are not rare. They are happening every day. Fathers come to court ready to parent and walk away feeling erased. They do not lose because they are unfit. They lose because the law allows decision-makers to act on personal opinions rather than consistent standards.

And this does not only hurt fathers. It hurts children who lose daily contact with a parent who is capable and loving. It hurts mothers who are asked to carry more than they should have to. And it hurts the legitimacy of a system that claims to serve families but often relies on tradition instead of fairness.

One might ask why appeals are not more common in these situations. The answer is simple. Custody rulings are usually seen as matters of discretion, not legal error. Unless a judge violates a clear legal rule or refuses to follow due process, appeals courts rarely overturn the decision. This makes it almost impossible for a father to challenge an unfair outcome. He must live with it. Or spend years and money trying to modify the order, often with little success.

What these stories show is that something is missing. That missing piece is a firm and fair starting point. When courts begin from a position of equal parenting, these outcomes become harder to justify. They require explanation. They require proof. And that pressure forces the court to think more carefully, more transparently, and more honestly about what is truly best for the child.

The Impact of Bias Even When Unintentional

Bias does not always arrive with bad intentions. It is not always loud or obvious. In fact, some of the most harmful forms of bias are quiet, and live in habits of thinking that go unchallenged. They hide in traditions that have never been questioned. And they shape decisions in ways that feel normal, even reasonable, to the person making them.

In family court, this kind of bias is especially dangerous because custody decisions rely heavily on personal judgment. There is no jury. There is no fixed formula. The judge listens to both sides and then decides what is best for the child. That is a heavy responsibility. But it is also an environment where unconscious bias can take root and grow.

Judges are human. They bring to the bench their education, their upbringing, their past cases, and their beliefs about families. Some have decades of experience in child welfare. Others come from criminal or civil law and are new to custody matters. All of them are shaped by the world around them.

Research in the field of cognitive psychology tells us that every human brain uses shortcuts to make sense of complex information. These shortcuts, known as cognitive biases, help people make quick decisions. But they can also lead to error. In a courtroom, this can mean favoring the more emotional witness. It can mean seeing a working father as less available. It can mean assuming that the parent who talks more is more involved. These are patterns, not facts. But they often go unexamined.

A 2019 study published in the *Family Court Review* explored how gender stereotypes influence custody decisions. The study found that judges often describe mothers in emotional terms and fathers in functional terms. Mothers were seen as nurturing. Fathers were seen as providers. These views, even when unspoken, affected how judges viewed parenting ability and time-sharing plans.

Another study by the American Bar Association found that even well-trained judges were vulnerable to implicit bias when making decisions under pressure. In custody cases, where emotions run high and facts are often disputed, those pressures are constant. Judges must sort through complicated personal histories, conflicting testimony, and vague standards. In that environment, unconscious bias can feel like instinct. But instinct is not law.

Consider a common example. A judge hears that the mother has handled most of the schoolwork and doctors' appointments. The father, while present, worked longer hours and handled fewer daily tasks. The judge may conclude that the mother should remain the primary parent. That conclusion may feel right. But what if both parents are now equally available? What if the father changed his schedule after separation? What if he is fully ready to co-parent? If the court fails to ask those questions, then the decision is not based on the present. It is based on an assumption drawn from the past.

Now imagine another scenario. A father becomes emotional in court. He raises his voice. He shows frustration. The judge sees this as a red flag. But a mother who cries may be seen as passionate and protective. These reactions are judged differently, even though both are emotional responses to stress. That is not fairness. That is bias in action.

The solution is not to blame judges. The solution is to build better systems. Judges should receive regular training on implicit bias, modern family structures, and child development. Courts should be required to write detailed findings when denying equal custody. Those findings should be grounded in facts, not impressions. And appellate courts should be more willing to review custody decisions when bias is suspected.

Another helpful step would be for states to collect and publish custody outcome data. That data should include information about parenting time awards, demographic patterns, and the frequency of equal parenting plans. With that information, researchers, lawmakers, and the public can begin to identify trends and demand change.

It is also important to change the courtroom culture. Lawyers should be encouraged to challenge assumptions without fear of disrespect. Parents should be allowed to explain their caregiving roles without being boxed into stereotypes. And judges should be given the support and tools they need to make decisions that are both fair and informed.

Unintentional bias is not a moral failure. It is a human limitation. But when that limitation affects a child's access to a parent, it becomes a legal failure. And the law must respond.

What Stanley v. Illinois Taught Us About Fathers' Rights

The United States Supreme Court does not often take family law cases. When it does, the decisions tend to carry enormous weight. That was the case in ***Stanley v. Illinois, 405 U.S. 645 (1972)***, a landmark ruling that still stands as one of the strongest affirmations of a father's constitutional right to parent his child.

Let us begin with the facts. Peter Stanley lived with his partner Joan for eighteen years. They had three children together. Though they were never legally married, they built a family life and raised their children as co-parents. When Joan died, the state of Illinois immediately declared the children wards of the state and placed them in foster care. Why? Because Peter was not legally married to Joan, the law classified him as an unfit parent without a hearing. He was given no chance to demonstrate that he had provided love, care, or support for his children.

Peter Stanley challenged the law. He argued that he had a right to raise his children and that the state could not simply presume him to be unfit based on marital status alone. The case went all the way to the Supreme Court.

The Court's ruling was clear and powerful. In a unanimous decision, the justices held that parents cannot be denied custody without due process. The Court recognized the bond between parent and child as a fundamental liberty interest protected by the Fourteenth Amendment. It stated that the state must treat unmarried fathers with the same respect it gives to other parents. Fitness must be proven, not assumed. And no parent may be treated as unfit unless given notice, a hearing, and a fair chance to respond.

This decision broke new ground. It dismantled the automatic presumption that unwed fathers were legally irrelevant. It reminded the country that parental rights are not based on status, but on commitment and care. And it placed constitutional limits on a state's ability to separate families without due process.

But the most powerful message of ***Stanley v. Illinois*** was this. The Court rejected the idea that the state knows better than the family. It held that a parent who has acted as a parent cannot be erased by law simply because they do not fit society's preferred mold. It was not a defense of biology alone. It was a defense of relationship, presence, and effort.

The ruling had immediate legal consequences. States across the country were forced to revise laws that denied rights to unmarried fathers. Family courts had to stop assuming that motherhood came with automatic custody while fatherhood had to be proven. The decision made clear that the Constitution protects all parents, not just those who check the right legal boxes.

Yet more than fifty years later, many of the challenges Peter Stanley faced still appear in modern form.

Fathers are still asked to prove their value. They are still seen as secondary unless they meet high and often vague standards. They are still denied equal time even when they have done nothing wrong. And they still face laws and court cultures that assume that caregiving and motherhood are the same thing.

So what lessons can we take from ***Stanley*** today?

First, we must expand the Court's logic to all custody decisions. If a father cannot be presumed unfit because he was not married, then a father also should not be presumed less important because he was not the primary caregiver during marriage. Courts must recognize the ongoing nature of parenting. Past roles do not dictate future capacity.

Second, we must understand that due process does not just mean having a day in court. It means having a fair chance to be heard. That includes fair access to legal representation, equal consideration of parenting plans, and the right to challenge false assumptions.

Third, we must recognize that fathers' rights are children's rights too. When courts protect a father's relationship with his child, they are also protecting the child's emotional well-being, sense of identity, and family stability. The Constitution does not protect parents in a vacuum. It protects the relationship, the bond, and the right to grow together.

Finally, we must not let ***Stanley*** remain just a case in a textbook. Its lessons must shape how we write laws, how we train judges, and how we talk about families. The Court gave us the principle. Now we must put it into practice.

Why Equal Custody Helps Children Not Just Fathers

One of the most common misunderstandings in the debate about equal parenting is the idea that it is about fathers trying to gain more rights for themselves. This view often frames the conversation as one parent versus the other. But equal custody is not about giving one parent more power. It is about giving children more connection, more security, and more love from both parents.

Children are not prizes to be won in a courtroom. They are human beings with emotional needs that go far beyond legal schedules. They need routine and support. They need someone to help with homework, to cook dinner, to take them to practice, and to tuck them in at night. And they need those things from both of their parents whenever possible.

Dozens of studies have shown that children who spend significant and regular time with both parents after separation do better in nearly every category of development. The National Institute for Mental Health has reported that children in shared custody arrangements show lower levels of depression and anxiety. A study published in the *Journal of Epidemiology and Community Health* found that children with equal parenting time had fewer psychosomatic problems than those who lived mostly with one parent.

Another major study, conducted by Dr. Linda Nielsen of Wake Forest University, reviewed forty academic papers on shared parenting. Her findings were clear. Children in joint physical custody arrangements had better outcomes in terms of academic achievement, family relationships, self-esteem, and emotional health. These benefits were not limited to high-income families or low-conflict parents. They held true across a wide range of situations.

Why does shared parenting work so well?

The first reason is emotional stability. When children know that both of their parents are actively involved and available, they feel more secure. They do not carry the burden of choosing sides. They do not feel abandoned or replaced. They grow up knowing that their family is still whole, even if it lives in two homes.

The second reason is role modeling. Children need to see how different adults handle challenges, emotions, responsibilities, and routines. Each parent brings unique strengths. One may be more structured. The other more flexible. One may focus on academics. The other on creativity. These differences are not problems. They are advantages. They help children learn resilience and adapt to real-life situations.

The third reason is consistency in discipline and values. When both parents are involved, they can share expectations and reinforce the same lessons. This avoids the common situation where one parent becomes the fun parent while the other is left with all the hard work. Equal parenting spreads both the joys and the duties of raising a child.

The fourth reason is protection against parental alienation. When one parent is sidelined or given minimal time, the relationship can weaken. Over time, that distance can turn into resentment or estrangement. But when both parents are regularly present, there is less chance for one to dominate or manipulate the child's view of the other.

Let us also consider the practical benefits. Equal custody often leads to better communication between parents. It encourages both parents to stay informed about school, medical care, and extracurricular activities. It can reduce the stress on one parent who would otherwise carry the full load of daily life. And it makes it more likely that parents will share financial responsibilities fairly.

Some critics argue that shared parenting only works when parents get along well. But research shows that even in moderate conflict cases, children still benefit from spending time with both parents, as long as the conflict is kept away from the child. In fact, a structured equal parenting plan can reduce conflict by removing the fear of losing access to the child.

Of course, there are cases where equal time is not possible or safe. No one argues that a child should be placed in danger or forced into a schedule that truly does not work. But those cases are the exception. They should not define the rule. The default should reflect what works for most families when both parents are capable and willing.

Equal custody is not a gift to fathers. It is a recognition of reality. In today's world, parenting is shared in marriage and it should be shared in separation. Children deserve the full love, wisdom, and presence of both parents. That is not a father's right or a mother's right. It is the child's right.

FOUR

Policy and Legislative Trends Toward Shared Parenting

For decades, custody laws across the United States have rested on one central idea: that the court should decide what is best for the child based on the facts of each case. This sounds fair. In theory, it gives judges flexibility. It allows decisions to be shaped by each family's unique circumstances. But in practice, this system has led to widespread inequality and confusion. Too often, what is called flexibility has become inconsistency. What is called discretion has become a doorway for bias. And what is supposed to serve children's interests has often ended up serving outdated views of parenting.

In recent years, lawmakers, researchers, and advocates have begun asking hard questions. Why should one parent start with more rights than the other when both are fit and willing? Why are parenting time decisions so different from one courtroom to another? Why are fathers still being pushed into the role of visitor when the evidence clearly shows children do better with two active parents?

These questions have led to change. In state after state, legislators have proposed and passed laws that shift the foundation of custody decisions. These laws do not take power away from judges. They do not put children in unsafe situations. What they do is create a new starting point. They say that unless there is a good reason not to, children should spend equal time with both parents.

Family law in the United States has long been left to the discretion of individual states. This means that custody laws, procedures, and outcomes vary widely from one jurisdiction to another. But in recent years, a powerful shift has been underway. State legislatures have begun to reconsider the traditional custody model in favor of something more balanced and fair. A growing number of states are passing or proposing laws that make shared parenting, not primary custody with one parent, the starting point.

This chapter explores how those changes have taken shape. It will look at real laws passed in real states and the results those laws have produced. It will compare states that embraced shared parenting with those that have resisted it. And it will offer a roadmap for how lawmakers and courts can move toward a custody system that is fairer, clearer, and more focused on what children truly need.

Comparing Outcomes Before and After Equal Parenting Laws

Laws are only as powerful as the change they bring. While policy debates often focus on what should happen in theory, families live with what actually happens in practice. That is why it is critical to ask a simple but important question. Do shared parenting laws work?

To answer that question, we must look at what changed in the states that adopted equal parenting presumptions. We must compare outcomes before and after those changes. We must study how courts responded, how parents behaved, and most importantly, how children were affected.

Let us begin with the state that led the way: Kentucky.

In 2018, Kentucky became the first state to pass a law that created a legal presumption of joint physical custody and equal parenting time at the temporary hearing stage in divorce and separation cases. That law was later expanded to apply to permanent custody decisions as well. The statute, ***KRS 403.280*** established a simple but powerful principle: when both parents are fit and willing, equal time is presumed to be in the best interest of the child.

The results were immediate and measurable. A 2021 report by the Kentucky Administrative Office of the Courts showed that the number of high-conflict custody cases dropped significantly. Fewer parents were returning to court to fight over modifications. More children were spending meaningful time with both parents. The law had reduced conflict and improved outcomes without increasing court burdens.

Inspired by Kentucky, several other states followed suit. Arkansas passed legislation creating a presumption of equal parenting time. Arizona had already implemented a strong shared parenting policy through judicial guidelines that prioritize substantial and frequent contact with both parents. In Florida, a recent bill established equal time sharing as the starting point unless evidence shows it would not be in the child's best interest.

Each of these states used a slightly different approach, but they all shared the same goal: to make equal custody the default assumption unless a compelling reason suggests otherwise.

Other states are now considering similar reforms. As of 2025, more than thirty states have introduced bills to create or expand shared parenting laws. Some of these efforts have stalled due to opposition from special interest groups, family law associations, or legislators who fear change. But public support remains strong. Polls conducted by the National Parents Organization and other advocacy groups consistently show that a large majority of Americans support equal parenting after divorce.

Why does this matter?

It matters because when laws change, systems follow. Judges who once relied on discretion must now justify deviations from equal time. Lawyers who once focused on winning primary custody now focus on crafting workable parenting plans. Parents who once fought out of fear of losing access to their child now begin from a place of security. And children gain the opportunity to grow up with both parents fully involved.

The movement toward equal parenting also aligns with broader trends in American law and policy. Workplace norms are changing. More fathers are taking on caregiving roles. More mothers are working full time. Gender roles are evolving. Families are diverse. The old model of one parent at home and one at work no longer applies to most households. The law must reflect that reality.

Shared parenting laws also save money. High-conflict custody battles are expensive. They clog courts, drain family resources, and cause emotional harm that lasts for years. When states implement equal parenting presumptions, they reduce the financial and emotional cost of family litigation. Parents reach agreements faster. Hearings are shorter. Enforcement is easier.

But these laws are not perfect. Implementation is needed. In some states, the language of shared parenting is vague. In others, the standard can be overcome too easily with vague concerns about logistics or vague references to instability. Courts still need clear guidance on how to apply these laws consistently and fairly.

To ensure the success of shared parenting reforms, states should take several important steps.

First, statutes must define the best interests of the child in clear and measurable terms. Factors should include the willingness of each parent to cooperate, the mental and physical health of the parents, the child's school and activity needs, and the history of involvement by each parent. Vague language should be avoided.

Second, courts must be required to explain themselves when they depart from equal parenting. A legal presumption only has power when it is enforced. If a judge decides that a child should not spend equal time with both parents, there must be a written explanation based on facts. This serves several purposes. It promotes fairness because both parents understand why the decision was made. It promotes trust because it shows the judge applied the law thoughtfully and not arbitrarily. And it provides a clear record for appellate courts to review. Without written findings, it is impossible to know whether the court acted within the law or outside of it. Transparency in decision-making is the first step toward accountability.

Third, legal reform is only as strong as the people applying it. Judges and attorneys need training that reflects the realities of modern parenting and the science of child development. Judicial training programs should include current research on the benefits of shared parenting, the importance of maintaining emotional bonds with both parents, and the impact of bias in custody decisions. Courts must also be educated on the changing roles of parents in society. The assumption that one parent works and the other raises the children is no longer the norm. Parenting responsibilities today are often shared long before separation. The legal system must catch up to that reality.

Fourth, states need to collect and publish data on how custody decisions are being made. Reform cannot be measured without evidence. States should track how often equal parenting is ordered, what factors are cited when the presumption is rebutted, how parenting time is distributed across different demographics, and what trends emerge in long-term outcomes. This data can help lawmakers identify which policies are working and which are not. It can also expose patterns of inconsistency or bias that may otherwise go unnoticed. Just as schools are held accountable through performance data, so too should family courts be accountable for the decisions they make about children's lives.

Fifth, while custody law is primarily governed by states, federal leadership still has an important role to play. Congress could support shared parenting by proposing model legislation that states can adapt. It could also create incentive programs similar to those used in the child support system. For example, states that adopt clear equal parenting statutes and meet transparency standards could qualify for federal funding to improve family court services. Federal agencies could also fund research into the long-term effects of shared parenting and offer grants for judicial training. Coordination at the national level would not replace state authority. It would support it with tools, knowledge, and encouragement toward fairer outcomes.

These reforms are not radical. They are rooted in law, supported by science, and shaped by experience. They reflect what many judges and lawyers already know but are not always empowered to act on. Shared parenting is not about giving parents equal time for its own sake. It is about giving children equal access to love, support, and stability from both of the people who brought them into the world.

But to understand the full impact of shared parenting laws, we must also examine what happens in states that have **not** adopted these reforms. The contrast is telling.

In many of these states, custody outcomes remain highly uneven. National data continues to show that where equal parenting is not the starting point, mothers are still awarded primary physical custody in more than **seventy percent** of contested cases. Fathers, even when fully capable and willing, are often granted minimal visitation, typically alternating weekends and perhaps a midweek dinner. This schedule does not reflect shared parenting. It reflects marginalization. And it offers little opportunity for fathers to form the deep, consistent bonds children need from both parents.

Importantly, this imbalance is not always the result of intentional discrimination. In many cases, judges are simply following patterns that have persisted for decades. Without a statute requiring them to begin from a place of equality, many courts rely on long-standing assumptions about caregiving roles. These assumptions often have more to do with cultural tradition than with modern reality or child development research.

Critics of shared parenting laws sometimes argue that such statutes limit judicial discretion or force rigid schedules. But every shared parenting law examined in this chapter includes clear exceptions. Judges retain full authority to deny equal parenting time when there is credible evidence of abuse, neglect, substance abuse, or serious instability. What the law changes is not judicial power. What it changes is the starting line.

Instead of forcing one parent, usually the father, to fight for time, these laws require evidence to deny that time. That is not an inflexible rule. It is a **fair and constitutional presumption** that both parents matter, unless proven otherwise.

Shared parenting laws also do not erase the voice of the child or override the need for customized arrangements. These laws do not mandate fifty-fifty parenting in every situation. They create a framework that *values balance*, that sets a *standard of fairness*, and that ensures both parents are treated as equally important from the outset. This allows courts to tailor outcomes to the child's specific needs without starting from a place of inequality.

The data is clear. When equal parenting becomes the default presumption, custody outcomes grow more balanced. Litigation decreases. Parents cooperate more. Children benefit. And the system functions more efficiently and transparently.

Shared parenting laws are not only legal reform. They are a **cultural correction** - a re-alignment of family law with modern realities, child-focused research, and the fundamental truth that children deserve both of their parents fully present in their lives.

What Worked What Did Not and Why

Shared parenting laws are changing the legal landscape across many states. But change alone is not the goal. The goal is progress that truly benefits children, parents, and the courts themselves. While some states have seen major success with shared parenting laws, others have faced challenges. To fully understand this legal evolution, we must ask what has worked, what has not, and why.

Let us begin with what has worked well.

One of the most consistent successes is the reduction in parental conflict. In states like *Kentucky*, where shared parenting became the default starting point, parents were less likely to fight each other in court. This is because when both parents know they are beginning from an equal position, there is less fear of losing access to their children. They do not need to prove the other parent is bad. They do not feel they must win in order to remain present in their child's life. This shift lowers tension and encourages cooperation.

Another area of success has been the growth in voluntary agreements. Before shared parenting laws, many cases turned into battles because the default expectation was that one parent would win primary custody. With equal time as the starting point, more parents have begun to create parenting plans together without waiting for a judge to decide. Mediation becomes more effective when both sides feel they have something to gain rather than something to lose.

Shared parenting laws have also helped judges. While some worried that these laws would limit their flexibility, many judges now say the opposite. The new laws give them a clear structure. They still have the power to make exceptions when needed, but the law provides a fair and balanced foundation that reduces guesswork and personal bias. Judges can focus on real problems rather than trying to decide which parent deserves more time based on unclear or outdated standards.

Another success is better outcomes for children. As covered earlier in this chapter, research shows that when children have regular and meaningful contact with both parents, they tend to perform better in school, have fewer behavioral issues, and build stronger relationships with both sides of their family. This benefit becomes more common when equal parenting is expected from the start and protected by law.

Now let us turn to what has not worked as well.

One of the biggest problems has been inconsistency in how the laws are applied. Even in states with strong shared parenting statutes, some judges still revert to old habits. They may still favor one parent without a strong reason or accept vague claims about logistics or emotional strain as reasons to deny equal time. This happens more often when the law does not require judges to give written explanations for their decisions. Without clear reasoning on the record, it becomes hard to appeal or challenge unfair outcomes.

Another issue is lack of education. Not every judge or attorney has been trained on how to apply shared parenting laws. Some still operate under the belief that equal time is only for low-conflict cases or that children need one primary home to feel stable. These beliefs may come from experience, but they often ignore new research and modern family structures. If the people applying the law do not understand the law's purpose, then reform can be slowed or blocked entirely.

Some states have passed shared parenting laws with language that is too vague. A law that simply encourages equal time without setting a clear presumption does not have much impact. It gives the appearance of reform but leaves too much to discretion. True change requires statutes that begin with a presumption of equal parenting and that clearly outline when and how that presumption can be overcome.

There have also been concerns in some states about how shared parenting applies in complex cases. For example, when parents live far apart or when children have special needs that require careful planning, equal time may not always be simple to arrange. But these concerns do not mean the law is wrong. They mean the law must be applied thoughtfully, with attention to detail and flexibility when needed. Courts must have the tools and resources to build custom parenting plans that still respect the principle of equality.

Lastly, there is the challenge of public misunderstanding. Some people believe shared parenting laws are designed to help fathers at the expense of mothers. Others think they are one-size-fits-all solutions that ignore unique family dynamics. These fears are often fueled by misinformation or lack of experience with how the laws actually work. What is needed is better public education about what shared parenting really means and how it serves the child first and foremost.

In summary, shared parenting laws work best when they are clear, consistently applied, supported by training, and grounded in real data. They work when courts require transparency and when judges are equipped to make thoughtful decisions. They work when the public understands that equality in parenting is not about helping one side win. It is about helping children thrive.

The Growing National Movement for Equal Custody

Across the United States, a powerful shift is taking place in how custody is understood, debated, and legislated. It began as a quiet call for fairness from a few advocacy groups and family law reformers but has now grown into a national movement that is changing laws, reshaping courtrooms, and redefining what it means to put children first.

This movement is not about pushing one parent aside. It is about rethinking the structure of post-separation parenting. It is about making sure that the law reflects the lives that modern families actually live. It is about moving beyond outdated assumptions and building a system where both parents are treated with equal dignity and children are given the stability of consistent relationships with both of the people who love and raise them.

At the heart of this movement are families. Fathers who have fought to stay involved in their children's lives. Mothers who believe that co-parenting is a strength, not a threat. Grandparents, educators, psychologists, and attorneys who have seen the emotional cost of a custody system that too often turns children into trophies. Their voices are louder now. Their experiences are shaping policy.

In state after state, equal parenting bills are being introduced. As of 2025, more than thirty states have considered or are actively working on legislation that would establish equal physical custody as the legal presumption. Some of these efforts are led by bipartisan coalitions of lawmakers who recognize that shared parenting is not a political issue but a family one. Others are driven by grassroots campaigns that gather thousands of signatures, organize public hearings, and bring real parents to testify about their experiences in court.

Groups like the National Parents Organization and Americans for Equal Shared Parenting have played a central role in this effort. They provide research, model legislation, and public awareness campaigns. They connect families across state lines. They make the case that shared parenting is supported not only by common sense but also by hard data and constitutional principle.

Their work has brought about real change. Laws have already passed in *Kentucky*, *Arkansas*, and *Florida*. In *Arizona*, judicial guidelines have effectively created a shared parenting framework even in the absence of a legislative mandate. Other states, including *Missouri*, *Texas*, *New York*, and *Michigan*, are actively debating similar reforms. The conversation is growing louder in courtrooms, legislative halls, law schools, and social media platforms.

The national movement is also gaining support from scholars and child development experts. Research consistently shows that children benefit from meaningful relationships with both parents. More professionals are speaking out in support of equal time. More courts are beginning to recognize that stability does not mean living mostly with one parent while visiting the other. Stability means knowing that both parents are there, involved, and committed.

Of course, the path forward is not without resistance. Some legal professionals worry that equal custody laws will take away discretion. Some parents worry that shared parenting will expose children to conflict. And there are still those who believe that traditional roles should guide parenting after divorce. But these concerns must be met with facts, compassion, and a clear understanding of what the law can do when it is properly applied.

The truth is that shared parenting laws do not create conflict. They reduce it. They do not favor one parent over the other. They level the playing field. And they do not ignore safety concerns. They make sure those concerns are addressed through evidence, not assumptions.

This is not just a legal reform. It is a cultural transformation. It is a rethinking of how families should be supported, not separated. And it is long overdue.

How Federal Policy Could Support State-Level Change

While family law has traditionally been governed by state legislatures and courts, there are moments in history when national leadership can help guide local reform. The movement for equal parenting is one of those moments. Although each state retains the authority to define its own custody laws, the federal government has tools that can promote fairness, consistency, and better outcomes across all fifty states.

One of the most important ways federal policy can help is through model legislation. Just as the federal government supported the development of uniform laws in areas like child support enforcement, it can now offer guidance on best practices for custody. A federal agency or congressional task force could work with child development experts, family law scholars, and judicial representatives to draft a clear and balanced model shared parenting statute. This statute could define key terms, establish a strong but rebuttable presumption of equal custody, and outline the evidentiary standards required to depart from that presumption.

Such a model would not override state law. Instead, it would give states a blueprint to follow. It would help prevent the current situation in which custody laws vary so widely that a parent's rights depend more on where they live than on what is best for the child.

In addition to legislation, federal funding could provide critical support for states that adopt shared parenting policies. Congress could establish grant programs that reward states for implementing equal custody laws with safeguards for child safety and judicial accountability. These grants could be used to expand mediation services, offer parenting education programs, and improve the technology that courts use to manage co-parenting schedules and communication between parents.

Federal agencies could also support research and data collection. A national database of custody outcomes would allow policymakers to compare states, identify trends, and evaluate the success of different approaches. With more data, states could better understand what factors influence judicial decisions, which communities experience the most inequality, and how changes in law affect the long-term well-being of children.

Another important area for federal support is judicial and legal training. The U.S. Department of Justice or the Department of Health and Human Services could develop training programs that help judges and lawyers understand the latest research on child development, co-parenting, and implicit bias. These programs could be offered through continuing legal education requirements or in partnership with law schools and judicial conferences.

Finally, national leadership can shape public understanding. When Congress holds hearings, issues reports, or passes resolutions in support of equal parenting, it sends a message that this issue matters. It tells the public that custody is not just a private matter but a national concern that affects millions of children. Public awareness leads to better laws, better parenting, and better outcomes.

The role of the federal government is not to take control but to provide structure, resources, and direction. By encouraging consistency and fairness in custody decisions, national policy can help ensure that children across the country have the same basic right to love and be loved by both parents.

With the support of federal leadership, the equal parenting movement can move from scattered victories to national reform. What began as a grassroots demand for fairness can become a lasting shift in how America understands family, justice, and childhood.

FIVE

Exceptional Circumstances When 50 50 Custody Should Not Apply

The movement toward equal custody is built on the belief that children benefit most when both parents are actively involved in their lives. The goal is fairness, stability, and most importantly, to promote the well-being of the child by ensuring that no loving and capable parent is removed or reduced without a strong reason.

However, no presumption should ever be absolute. Law must be flexible enough to account for the realities of human behavior and family complexity. While equal parenting is a strong and fair starting point in most cases, it cannot be the final answer in all cases. There are situations in which shared custody may expose a child to harm, instability, or unnecessary emotional stress. These situations must be taken seriously. The legal system must remain vigilant in protecting the most vulnerable party in any custody dispute: the child.

This chapter explores those exceptions. It examines when and how courts can and should depart from the equal parenting presumption. It addresses questions like what counts as a legitimate concern, how the courts can verify claims of unfitness or abuse, and what legal standards must be met before a parent's time with their child is restricted.

Importantly, this chapter also highlights the danger of vague or unproven allegations. While the law must protect children, it must also protect against false claims or emotional arguments that are not supported by evidence. We will look at how courts can balance the need for safety with the need for fairness, and how a strong evidentiary standard, such as clear and convincing proof can help ensure that exceptions to equal parenting are applied only when truly necessary.

This is not a chapter that opposes shared custody. Rather, it strengthens the case for shared custody by acknowledging its limits. A good legal system does not pretend that all families look the same. It recognizes risk. It investigates facts. And it applies the law in a way that reflects both justice and compassion.

We will draw from real case law, such as rulings involving abuse, substance dependency, severe mental illness, or a history of neglect. We will also explore the safeguards that are already in place through laws like the ***Uniform Child Custody Jurisdiction and Enforcement Act (UCCJEA)***, and we will propose ideas for improving how courts assess parental fitness without falling into bias or speculation.

Most parents are capable of co-parenting when given the right tools and a fair legal environment. But for those rare but critical cases in which shared parenting would endanger a child's well-being, the law must remain strong and clear.

When Equal Parenting Should Not Apply

Shared custody is not about creating a perfect 50:50 balance in every case. It is about starting from the assumption that both parents are equally important unless proven otherwise. But sometimes, equal parenting is not appropriate. Some children face real risks that make shared custody harmful. These risks include exposure to abuse, neglect, untreated mental illness, and severe substance dependency. In such cases, courts have a duty to place safety above all else.

That does not mean the court should abandon fairness or jump to conclusions. It means the law must allow space to prioritize the child's safety and stability when credible and serious concerns exist. But these concerns must be proven. The starting point should be equal custody, but when that outcome could clearly harm the child, courts must be empowered to step away from it.

The key is that the decision to do so must be rooted in real evidence. Not suspicions. Not general fears. Not outdated assumptions. Real facts, professionally evaluated, and fairly presented.

50:50 is the fair starting point for most families. But every legal principle must allow for exceptions. These exceptions must not be assumed. They must be proven. And when they are justified, they must be applied with care, precision, and clear evidence. Children should never be placed in environments that endanger their mental or physical well-being. Just as the system must protect the rights of both parents, it must first and foremost protect the rights and safety of the child.

One of the strongest justifications for departing from equal custody is abuse. If a parent has a history of domestic violence or child abuse, the court must act with urgency and caution. In these cases, shared parenting may not be safe. However, the court must base its decisions on actual evidence and findings, not on allegations alone. Too often, custody battles devolve into emotional accusations, many of which are unverifiable or used strategically. This is dangerous not only for the accused parent but for the integrity of the court and for the child who may be manipulated or placed in emotional turmoil.

That is why courts should apply a high standard of proof in such cases. Clear and convincing evidence should be the required threshold for rebutting the presumption of equal custody. This standard is higher than a preponderance of the evidence but lower than beyond a reasonable doubt. It allows the court to act decisively when the risk is real while protecting against bias, assumptions, and unfair outcomes based on speculation.

In addition to abuse, substance dependency is another area that may justify limiting a parent's time. If a parent struggles with addiction to drugs or alcohol and is not receiving treatment, then the court must consider the impact on the child's safety and daily care. However, here too, the court must be careful. Addiction is a medical condition. A parent in recovery who is following a treatment plan, maintaining sobriety, and showing commitment to their child should not be automatically excluded. Courts must distinguish between current, active risk and past struggles that are being responsibly addressed.

Mental illness can also be a concern, but it must be examined with care. A diagnosis alone should not be used to deny custody. Many people with mental health conditions live full and stable lives. The question should not be whether a parent has a diagnosis but whether their condition currently affects their ability to parent safely and responsibly. Courts should consult medical professionals and not rely on stigma or assumptions.

Neglect and abandonment are also relevant. If a parent has shown a consistent pattern of absence or unwillingness to care for the child, then the presumption of equal time can be rebutted. Still, the court must look at the reasons behind the absence. Some parents are pushed away by legal systems that do not support their involvement. Some are financially unable to access legal representation. A history of limited involvement must be understood in context.

Distance and logistical complications may also come into play. If one parent lives far from the child's school or the other parent's home, then a traditional week on and week off schedule may not work. But instead of eliminating shared custody, courts should look for creative solutions. This might include long weekends, school holidays, or virtual communication when in-person visits are limited. Equal parenting does not mean identical schedules. It means equal effort to maintain a meaningful relationship.

In all of these exceptions, the principle must remain the same. The decision to deny equal parenting must be based on facts, not fears. The evidence must be real. And the burden of proof must rest with the parent or party seeking to exclude the other. Equal parenting should remain the starting point. Departure from that point must be explained, documented, and reviewed if necessary.

At this point, I must also say something clearly. I am not calling for a toxic chant that arms fathers to act as if they are always the victims. That would be irresponsible. There are fathers who are dangerous.

There are fathers who should not have custody. The system must remain firm in removing harmful influences from a child's life when those influences are proven to exist. But the problem is that many good fathers are being treated as if they are bad simply because they are fathers. They are grouped into a category they do not belong to. That is what we must change.

We must separate the good from the dangerous with care and intelligence. We cannot afford to protect children from one risk while exposing them to another, the loss of a loving and involved parent. The law must be strong enough to protect against violence and neglect but wise enough to support the presence of nurturing fathers who want to be there.

To do this, courts need more than statutes. They need tools. Expert evaluators must be trained not only in psychology but in identifying false claims. Parenting coordinators should be used to help families navigate transitions safely. Judges should receive training on trauma and abuse but also on how to identify manipulation, exaggeration, and misuse of protective laws.

In addition, courts must issue detailed findings when they deny equal parenting. Vague phrases like it is not in the best interest of the child are not enough. The decision must explain what facts support that conclusion. If a parent is denied equal time, the judgment must identify what behaviors led to that result and whether those behaviors can be addressed. This gives both accountability and hope. It also allows appellate courts to review and correct mistakes when necessary.

Finally, we must talk about supervision and graduated parenting plans. In cases where a parent has a concerning history but shows signs of improvement, courts should not automatically shut the door. Instead, they should create parenting plans that allow for monitored time with clear goals and milestones. If the parent progresses, their time can be increased. This balances safety with restoration and avoids permanent loss based on past conduct that may be correctable.

The law must never confuse caution with cruelty. To protect children, we must act with precision, with compassion, and with courage. That means giving equal custody when it is deserved and denying it only when the facts demand it.

Let's now look closely at the legal tools already in place to support these exceptions and, examine how statutes like the ***Uniform Child Custody Jurisdiction and Enforcement Act*** work, and what more can be done to ensure that courts act wisely and justly in the rare but serious cases where equal custody is not appropriate.

How Courts Use Legal Tools to Justify Exceptions to Equal Custody

The law must always be flexible enough to respond to individual cases. That is why shared parenting laws include room for exceptions. These exceptions are not loopholes. They are safety mechanisms. Courts are allowed to move away from equal custody, but only when they have strong and reliable reasons to do so. This section looks at how those decisions are made and what legal tools courts use to guide and justify them.

One of the most important tools available to courts is the ***Uniform Child Custody Jurisdiction and Enforcement Act***, known as the UCCJEA. This law helps courts decide which state has the authority to rule on a custody matter. It prevents parents from taking children across state lines to get a different legal result. It also allows states to work together when there are questions of child safety or emergency custody. The UCCJEA ensures that one court handles the case, which helps reduce confusion and protects children from being moved around without structure or supervision.

Although the UCCJEA mainly deals with jurisdiction, it also supports exceptions to shared parenting by creating a space where safety is treated as a priority. For example, if a child has been subjected to or threatened with mistreatment, the court in the child's home state can quickly step in and create temporary orders to protect that child. This ensures that urgent cases do not get lost in legal delays.

Another tool courts use is the requirement of a "best interests" finding. While we have already discussed the need for this phrase to be clearly defined, it still plays a critical role in custody exceptions. When a judge believes equal custody would harm the child, the judge must explain how the proposed arrangement would not meet the child's needs. The best interests test must not be treated as a blank check. Instead, courts should point to specific facts. For example, a judge might find that one parent has no stable housing, a violent partner, or untreated mental health issues. These facts can justify a temporary or permanent limit on that parent's custody time.

Courts also rely on child custody evaluations, sometimes called forensic evaluations. These evaluations are conducted by psychologists or social workers who investigate the family and provide recommendations to the court. While these reports can be useful, they must be used carefully. A custody evaluator is not a judge. Their role is to offer insights, not to replace legal standards. Judges should not rely solely on these reports. Instead, the reports should be weighed against the evidence, the law, and the rights of both parents.

Guardian ad litem programs also play a role. A guardian ad litem is a court-appointed advocate for the child. This person speaks to the child, interviews parents and teachers, and provides an independent opinion to the court. While guardians can help ensure that the child's voice is heard, their recommendations must also be reviewed for fairness. No guardian is free from bias. Their opinions should never carry more weight than the law allows.

In some cases, courts use supervised visitation as a tool when full custody is not safe but some contact is still allowed. A parent who poses a risk to the child may be ordered to spend time with the child only in the presence of a neutral third party. This protects the child while giving the parent a chance to demonstrate change. Supervised visits can also be used temporarily when the facts are unclear and the court is still gathering evidence.

Restraining orders and protective orders are another tool. If one parent has threatened or harmed the child or the other parent, courts can issue orders that restrict contact. These orders can be short-term or long-term, depending on the severity of the situation. However, courts must also ensure that protective orders are not misused as tactics in custody fights. Each order should be based on facts, not on fear or strategy.

Most importantly, courts are expected to write findings of fact when they limit equal custody. This means they must list the reasons for their decision in writing. If a judge gives one parent more time than the other, the judge must explain why. These written findings protect everyone. They give the losing parent a chance to understand the decision. They give appellate courts a way to review the outcome. And they help prevent decisions that are based on personal opinion rather than legal standards.

What courts must avoid is the habit of making vague statements. Saying that equal custody is not in the best interest of the child is not enough. Saying that the child would be stressed without one primary home is not enough. The court must point to facts. Did one parent fail to show up to school events for a year? Was there police involvement for family violence? Did a therapist confirm emotional abuse? These are the types of facts that justify exceptions.

In addition to legal tools already in use, courts would benefit from new guidelines that help standardize how exceptions are handled. States could publish manuals that define when supervised visitation is appropriate, when mental health records should be reviewed, and how to assess parenting ability without bias. Training should be mandatory for all judges handling custody cases. Too much is at stake for the law to be applied without care.

At the same time, courts must also understand that denying a child access to a loving parent is a serious act. That decision should never be taken lightly. The emotional damage that comes from being cut off from a parent is real. It must be weighed just as carefully as any claim of risk. Courts have many tools to ensure children are safe when shared custody is not appropriate. These tools work best when applied with fairness, evidence, and transparency. The goal should never be to punish a parent. The goal should be to protect the child while keeping both parents involved whenever possible.

What Courts Look for in Cases of Abuse or Neglect

In cases of suspected abuse or neglect, courts are expected to examine a wide range of evidence before deciding whether to limit one parent's time with the child. They look for patterns in police reports, findings in child protective services investigations, testimony from professionals such as teachers, counselors, or pediatricians, and in some cases, direct statements from the child.

Physical abuse may leave visible marks or medical records. Emotional abuse may show up in school performance or psychological evaluations. Neglect may appear as repeated missed medical appointments, poor hygiene, lack of school attendance, or failure to meet the child's daily needs. Courts also consider the parent's past history. A criminal record involving domestic violence, drug-related charges, or repeated child welfare complaints can all raise serious concerns.

But one incident or one accusation should not automatically disqualify a parent. Judges must assess not just whether something happened, but how serious it was, how recent it was, whether it continues, and whether it shows a pattern of dangerous behavior. The goal is not to punish mistakes. It is to protect children from real and ongoing harm.

Understanding the Role of Evidence, Not Allegations

Too often, the mere presence of an accusation leads to unfair outcomes. Family court is particularly vulnerable to this problem because of its emotional nature. When parents are in conflict, they sometimes make claims that cannot be easily verified. They may exaggerate past behavior or interpret parenting disagreements as abuse. In some cases, one parent may make false allegations to gain leverage in the custody process.

That is why evidence is so important. A claim made without documentation, witness support, or professional evaluation should not be the sole basis for denying equal custody. This does not mean the court should ignore serious allegations. It means the court should pause, investigate, and weigh the claim against other facts. Temporary protective measures, such as supervised visitation or child interviews, can be used while the court gathers more information.

When decisions are made based on unproven claims, everyone loses. The child may lose access to a loving parent. The accused parent may be unfairly removed from the child's life. And the accusing parent may be rewarded for dishonesty, which damages the credibility of future victims who need the court's protection.

How the UCCJEA Guides Cross-State Custody and Protection

The ***Uniform Child Custody Jurisdiction and Enforcement Act*** is a legal framework adopted by nearly every state in the United States. Its goal is to reduce conflicts between states over custody decisions and to make sure children are not moved around unfairly when legal disputes arise.

The UCCJEA sets rules about which state has the authority to decide a custody matter. Usually, it is the child's home state, meaning where the child has lived for the past six months or longer. This prevents one parent from taking the child to another state in search of a more favorable ruling. It also creates a process for courts in different states to communicate with each other if a custody issue crosses state lines.

The UCCJEA is especially important in cases of emergency. If a child is in danger, courts in other states can issue temporary orders to protect them. However, these orders must still respect the rights of the other parent and defer to the home state's long-term authority when appropriate. This balance helps protect children without encouraging forum shopping or legal manipulation.

The act also supports enforcement. If one parent violates a custody order by taking the child to another state, the court in that new state can enforce the original order. This helps maintain stability for the child and discourages one parent from taking unilateral action.

Setting the Right Legal Threshold, Why "Clear and Convincing" Matters

When a court considers whether to deny equal custody, it must apply the right standard of proof. The best standard in these cases is "clear and convincing evidence." This standard is higher than the ordinary civil standard of "more likely than not," but lower than the criminal standard of "beyond a reasonable doubt." It requires that the court be firmly convinced of the truth of the claims being made.

Using this higher threshold respects what is at stake. Parenting time is not a small privilege. It is a fundamental part of a parent's relationship with their child. Taking that away should not be done lightly. The clear and convincing standard ensures that only well-substantiated and serious concerns can override the presumption of equal time.

This standard also protects the child from being used as a pawn in legal battles. It prevents judges from making custody decisions based on gut feelings or personal bias. It demands real evidence, presented clearly and tested fairly. And it gives appellate courts a strong framework to review decisions for fairness.

Protecting Children Without Abandoning Fairness

Some may worry that by focusing on fairness to both parents, we risk putting children in harm's way. That fear is understandable. But it is based on a misunderstanding. Protecting children and respecting parents are not opposing goals. They can and must go together.

Children are safest when the legal system is balanced, transparent, and evidence-based. They are safest when courts carefully investigate claims of danger but do not automatically assume guilt. They are safest when both parents are held to the same standards, and when the system supports healing and accountability rather than exclusion and punishment without cause.

The truth is that children suffer when good parents are removed from their lives without reason. They also suffer when dangerous parents are allowed too much access. The solution is not to tip the scale one way or the other. It is to build a system that applies the law with integrity and care.

Protecting children requires courage, knowledge, and humility. It requires judges to be trained in child development, trauma, and the effects of parental alienation. It requires lawyers to present facts, not just fears. And it requires lawmakers to write statutes that support fairness while providing strong tools to address danger when it exists.

The future of custody law must reflect this balance. Equal parenting should be the foundation. Exceptions should be allowed, but only when justified. And the process of making those exceptions must be transparent, rigorous, and grounded in facts.

Only then will we have a system that truly serves children by protecting their safety without sacrificing their right to be fully loved by both parents.

SIX

Public Opinion and Cultural Narratives in Custody Law

Family law does not exist in a vacuum. It grows out of the society it serves. It is shaped by the culture, attitudes, and stories people believe about parenting, gender roles, and what makes a good family. Even when the law is written with fairness in mind, it is often interpreted through the lens of public opinion and deep-rooted social assumptions.

In this chapter, we look at the invisible forces that shape custody outcomes before any parent steps foot in a courtroom. We explore how media stories, cultural expectations, and even outdated television portrayals of family life influence the way judges, lawyers, and everyday people think about mothers, fathers, and children. We ask how society came to assume that mothers are always the better parent or that fathers are less emotionally important. And we explore how these assumptions affect real legal outcomes for families.

This is a critical piece of the puzzle. Because until we change the way people think about parenting, it will be difficult to fully change the way custody law is applied. Legal reform and cultural reform must go hand in hand. It is not enough to rewrite statutes. We must also reshape the story that families and courts tell about themselves.

We begin by examining the most common myths that drive public opinion. Then we move into a discussion about how the media, school systems, and even workplace policies reinforce old ideas about who parents are and what roles they should play. Finally, we explore how cultural narratives can be transformed and how public education and advocacy can help build a more balanced and realistic understanding of parenting in the modern world.

Let's unpack the myths that influence the courtroom long before any legal argument is made.

The Myths That Shape Custody Decisions

Public opinion matters more than many people realize when it comes to how courts operate. Judges are expected to follow the law and make decisions based on evidence, but like everyone else, they live within a cultural system. They absorb the same messages from television, news, films, and public conversations. These messages can shape how they see fathers, mothers, and the idea of parenting itself.

One of the most harmful myths in family law is that mothers are naturally better caregivers. This belief is often unspoken. It rarely appears in official rulings. But it shows up in small ways. When a judge believes a mother should be the main parent unless proven otherwise. When an attorney tells a father not to expect more than weekends. When family or friends encourage a man not to fight for custody because he will lose anyway. All of these ideas come from the same outdated belief system.

This myth is not supported by science. Research in child development shows that children form strong emotional attachments with both parents. A father who changes diapers, reads bedtime stories, and walks his child to school plays just as meaningful a role as a mother who does those things. Parenting is not defined by gender. It is defined by presence, care, and love. Yet the belief that fathers are secondary continues to affect outcomes.

Another myth is that equal parenting creates instability. Critics argue that switching between homes will confuse children or leave them without a clear sense of structure. But studies have repeatedly shown that what children need most is a strong relationship with both parents.

Transitions between homes can be managed with planning and support. What causes stress is unpredictability and conflict, not shared time itself.

There is also the myth that equal custody encourages conflict between parents. The truth is often the opposite. When both parents know they will have equal time, there is less incentive to fight. The custody battle becomes less about winning and more about cooperation. Shared parenting laws reduce court battles because they start from a fair middle ground.

Finally, there is the dangerous idea that fighting for custody is somehow selfish. When fathers speak up about wanting equal time, they are sometimes told to put the child first. But asking to be part of your child's daily life is not selfish. It is responsible. Children deserve a strong bond with both parents. Denying that bond without cause is what truly harms them.

How Media and Institutions Reinforce Bias

The media plays a huge role in shaping public opinion. In popular films and television shows, mothers are usually shown as the primary caregivers. Fathers, when present, are often the comic relief, the outsider, or the disciplinarian. Rarely are they shown as equals in emotional caregiving. These portrayals influence how people think about real families. They set a cultural expectation that mothers belong in the home and fathers belong at work or at the edge of the child's life.

Schools and healthcare systems often do the same. Forms still ask for the mother's contact before the father's. Teachers sometimes assume that mothers are the ones managing the child's education. Doctors ask mothers more questions during appointments. These small signals build a picture that parenting is a mother's job, and fathers are visitors.

A recent podcast episode i saw this week captured this dynamic perfectly. A father described how, despite being actively involved in his child's life, nearly every message from the school began with 'Dear Mom' or 'Hi Mom.' None were addressed to him. He joked about it during the discussion, but it reflected a deeper disappointment. It was a reminder that even when fathers are present and committed, institutions often act as if they are invisible. His simple question captured the heart of the issue: 'Even if I'm not the one you expect, why not make room for the possibility that I might be?' These overlooked details reinforce the myth that fathers are secondary, and that must change.

Even workplace policies can reflect these beliefs. Many companies offer maternity leave but only limited paternity leave. Some managers still believe that mothers need more flexibility than fathers. This reinforces the idea that mothers are the primary parents and fathers are optional.

All of these cultural signals show up in court. Judges are human. They absorb the same assumptions. When no clear custody law demands equal treatment, cultural bias fills the gap. And fathers pay the price.

Changing the Narrative - Building a Culture of Equality

If we want the law to treat both parents fairly, we must also change the public conversation about parenting. This means telling new stories. It means highlighting fathers who are loving, present, and responsible. It means encouraging mothers who support shared custody to speak out. It means teaching children from an early age that parenting is not about gender. It is about love and responsibility.

Schools can help by involving both parents equally. Healthcare providers can help by always addressing both parents in medical decisions. Workplaces can support the change by offering equal parental leave. The media can do its part by portraying modern families where both parents are present and equally involved.

Family law conferences and continuing education courses can include sessions on cultural narratives. Law schools can teach students how unconscious bias shapes court decisions. Government agencies can run public awareness campaigns explaining that shared parenting is safe, stable, and healthy for children.

None of these changes happen overnight. But they matter. Because every custody case begins long before the courtroom. It begins with what the judge believes. What the lawyer expects. And what the parents think is even possible.

A Balanced Future

Equal custody is not only a legal reform. It is also a cultural correction. It challenges a long history of unequal parenting assumptions and offers a new standard built on evidence, fairness, and human dignity. While laws can mandate shared parenting, the true success of equal custody depends on whether society is willing to fully embrace a different story about family. That story must begin with a simple but powerful belief: that children need both of their parents. Not one more than the other. Not one by default. But both, equally and consistently.

To create a truly balanced future, we must first recognize how far the imbalance has reached. In many places, family courts still reflect the idea that mothers should be the primary caregivers and fathers should simply visit. This belief does not come from science or child psychology. It comes from generations of tradition, from a time when most families had one breadwinner and one caregiver. But families have changed. Gender roles have shifted. And the research is now overwhelming. Children who grow up with meaningful and consistent access to both parents do better in nearly every measurable way. They perform better academically. They have better emotional regulation. They experience lower rates of depression and anxiety. They develop healthier views of relationships. These are not theories. These are facts, documented through decades of research.

Despite this, many custody decisions still reduce one parent to a background role. Often that parent is the father. This is not always intentional. It is sometimes the result of subtle assumptions, outdated forms, or quiet pressure from friends and family. But the result is still the same. A child loses something essential. They are told, without words, that one of their parents matters less. That one is replaceable. That love and presence are somehow one-sided. And the damage this causes is not just emotional. It leaves a mark that can shape how that child views their own role as a parent in the future.

To move forward, we need more than new statutes. We need new stories. We need media that shows fathers and mothers working together to raise healthy, balanced children. We need schools that call both parents when a concern arises. We need doctors who ask both parents about the child's health. We need workplaces that support equal parenting leave. Every institution that touches the life of a child must reflect the value of both parents.

We must also support mothers who believe in shared parenting. Equal custody is not a threat to women. It is not about taking away rights. It is about recognizing that in many cases, mothers and fathers are equally capable, equally loving, and equally necessary. When the law starts from that understanding, it takes pressure off of both parents. It invites cooperation rather than competition. And it gives children the stability they deserve.

This conversation is not about defending one gender. It is not about saying all fathers are good or all mothers are favored. It is about understanding that family law should not operate from assumptions. It should operate from facts. And it should begin from a place of balance.

We must also be willing to talk about the pain that silence creates. There are thousands of fathers who do everything they can to be present. They attend school events. They rearrange work schedules. They drive hours to attend a weekend visit. Yet they are often told, directly or indirectly, that they do not matter as much. This is wrong. And it is preventable. At the same time, there are mothers who carry the full emotional and logistical load of parenting and feel unsupported by the system. This too is wrong. And it is also preventable.

True shared parenting gives every family member room to breathe. It says to the child, both of your parents matter. You do not have to choose. You do not have to lose one to keep the other. You are allowed to be fully loved by both.

Courts must reflect that belief. But so must culture. Because when culture supports shared parenting, the courts will follow. Legal change always runs deeper and lasts longer when society is ready to embrace it.

The opposite is also true. When the public still believes in old myths, even the best laws can be misused or misunderstood.

That is why we must be brave. Brave enough to challenge assumptions. Brave enough to listen to both parents. Brave enough to say that the role of a father is not secondary. That the love of a mother is not exclusive. And that children are not better off when love is divided. They are better off when love is shared.

A balanced future is not only possible. It is necessary. It begins with facts. It grows through education. And it is sustained by laws and institutions that reflect the dignity of both parents and the full humanity of every child.

Final Reflection and Policy Recommendations

As we reach the end of this book, it's important that we pause and reflect on what we have learned and why it matters. We have examined the principle of equal custody and the exceptional cases in which it may not apply. We have discussed the serious risks that some children face and the duty of courts to step in when a parent poses a threat. We have looked at how judges use legal tools like statutes, evidence, expert evaluations, and judicial discretion to navigate these difficult questions.

What becomes clear is this. The goal of any custody system should not be to choose a winner and a loser. It should not be to hand out parenting rights as a prize for good courtroom performance. The true goal is to build a plan that protects the child while honoring the bond between the child and both parents. This balance is not easy to achieve. But it is essential if the law is to be just.

In our current system, too many families are being divided unfairly. Too many fathers are losing contact with their children not because they are unfit but because the law does not begin with the right foundation. Too many courts are still operating on the assumption that one parent must do most of the raising while the other parent becomes a visitor. And in too many cases, exceptions to shared custody are made without real evidence or a clear explanation.

We must do better.

The first recommendation is that states must require written findings for every custody decision that departs from equal time. If a judge believes a parent should not have fifty percent custody, that decision must be explained in writing. The judge must identify the specific facts that led to that conclusion. This one change would dramatically improve accountability. It would force judges to rely on real data and real behavior rather than instinct or tradition. It would also give the other parent a clear path to appeal or seek improvement.

Second, courts should apply the standard of clear and convincing evidence before denying a fit parent equal time. This standard is already used in other serious family law matters, such as the termination of parental rights. It strikes the right balance. It does not demand absolute certainty, but it does require more than a casual assumption. It respects the gravity of what is at stake.

Third, the legal system must invest in training. Judges, lawyers, custody evaluators, and guardians ad litem should receive regular and mandatory education in trauma-informed care, implicit bias, child psychology, and shared parenting research. Without training, even the best laws can be misapplied. Training gives the system the tools it needs to adapt, respond, and grow.

Fourth, states should collect and publish data on custody decisions. This includes how often equal custody is awarded, what reasons are given for departures, and how outcomes differ based on race, gender, location, and income. Data allows for analysis. Analysis leads to reform. And transparency builds trust.

Fifth, courts should move toward restorative parenting plans in cases where one parent has made mistakes but shows a willingness to change. Instead of cutting a parent off forever, the law should create a path back to equal custody if certain goals are met. These goals might include attending counseling, maintaining sobriety, completing parenting classes, or participating in supervised visitation. Parents are not perfect. They can fail and still be worth saving. If a parent is dangerous, they must be kept away. But if a parent is struggling and improving, the law should leave room for healing and reunion.

Sixth, and this is deeply important, we must be careful not to build systems that punish fathers as a group. I am not suggesting that all fathers are victims. There are fathers who are abusive, neglectful, or absent by choice. These men must be removed from their children's lives until or unless they change. But we cannot use the existence of these men to justify the exclusion of others. A good father should not be judged by the worst examples. He should be evaluated on his own merit, his own record, and his own efforts. His child should not grow up wondering where he went when he was there all along waiting to be included.

When we talk about protecting children, we must also remember that losing a good parent is a form of harm. A child needs love, support, presence, and identity. These things are built through time. Through bedtime stories, school pickups, shared meals, hard conversations, and simple routines. When a child is denied these moments with a willing parent, something is taken from them that cannot be replaced.

The law must not only protect children from danger. It must also protect their right to be fully loved.

That means building laws that start from equality but remain flexible. It means using evidence, not emotion. It means training judges to recognize real risk while avoiding unconscious bias. And it means respecting the voices of families who live with the consequences of these decisions every single day.

This is not just a policy debate. It is a matter of human dignity. A matter of fairness. And a matter of national importance.

As we come to a close, we do so not with a final answer but with a renewed commitment to getting it right. Shared parenting is the future of custody law. But for that future to work, it must include both wisdom and compassion. It must protect the vulnerable without punishing the innocent. And it must always keep one question at the center of every decision.

Afterword

The pages of this book have walked through the law, the courtroom, the culture, and the heart of parenting. At its center stands one simple truth. Children do best when they are allowed to be loved by both of their parents. Not on a schedule that reduces one to a guest and the other to a gatekeeper. Not under a system that assigns value by tradition or stereotype. But in a structure that sees parenting as a shared responsibility and a shared right.

Family law is not just a legal field. It is where the law meets the kitchen table. It is where people go not to win arguments but to find a path forward. Too often, that path becomes a battlefield. Too often, children are caught between fear, bias, and outdated rules that were never designed for the world we live in today.

This book has argued for shared parenting not as a slogan but as a principle grounded in constitutional law, in scientific research, and in lived human experience. It is not an abstract theory. It is a response to what is happening in real courtrooms and real homes every day.

It has also acknowledged what some may be afraid to say out loud. That bias still exists. That good fathers are sometimes treated as optional. That the phrase best interest of the child has too often become a shield behind which unequal systems hide. And that the weight of the law has not been distributed fairly for all.

Still, we do not stand without hope.

Change is already happening. States are rewriting laws. Judges are rethinking old assumptions. Parents are speaking up. Advocates are building movements. And children are growing into adults who will expect better.

The next steps are not simple, but they are clear. The law must begin with equality, not exception. Courts must demand evidence, not assumption. Policymakers must listen not only to professionals but to families who live these struggles every day. And culture must follow the truth, that good parenting has never belonged to one gender, one role, or one stereotype.

To the fathers reading this, know that your love and presence matter more than any courtroom ruling can define. To the mothers reading this, know that equality does not diminish your role. It honors it by expecting the same from both parents. To the judges and lawyers reading this, know that every decision shapes a child's future. May your choices always be guided by fairness and courage. And to every child at the center of these cases, even when you cannot speak for yourself, may the adults around you finally build a system that listens to your needs with honesty and care.

We are not writing only about custody. We are writing about childhood. About love. About justice. And about the power of law to reflect not just what has been, but what should be.

Let this book be a beginning, a tool, a reminder, and a shared commitment to do better. Not just for fathers. Not just for mothers. But for the children who deserve both.Fully. Equally. Without condition.

www.ingramcontent.com/pod-product-compliance
Lightning Source LLC
LaVergne TN
LVHW022310200926
848481LV00004B/1272
* 9 7 9 8 2 9 5 5 3 7 3 2 5 *